THE SACRED WILL

OF THE PEOPLE

Works by **HUBERT TEMBA:**

Books:

1. Passages of Love

2. The Sacred Will Of The People

3. Jewels And Pearls, Petals and Roses, Venus And The Moon

4. Rivers Of Eternal Spring – (a motivational and inspirational essay in a book.)

Musical Productions and CDs:

1. Rhythms of Love

2. Flyin' High (In Ecstacy)

3. Let Me And My Guitars Rock You Down (To The Ground)

4. Songs From The Driver's Seat

5. Five Years In Paradise

6. When A Woman Is In Love She's Prettier Than Pretty

7. Angels

Library of Congress Cataloging-in-Publication Data

Temba, Hubert

The Sacred Will Of The People: an academic-oriented report about the tragedy of one socialistic experiment. This thesis is hinged on the use of mass persuasion in the implementation and demise of socialism in Tanzania, East Africa/Hubert Temba.

ISBN 1438210140

1. The Sacred Will Of The People

1. Title

EAN-13 is 9781438210148

TABLE OF CONTENTS Page Number

6

7

[7]

ABOUT THE AUTHOR

Thinker, philosopher, writer, composer, musicians et al was born on the slopes of Mount Kilimanjaro, in the north eastern part of Tanzania where his tribe, the *Chaggas,* have been nicknamed the Jews of Tanzania by some leading African States men.

Hubert Temba attended the University of Nairobi after which he was in the top six per cent of his graduating class with a writer-oriented Diploma of the School of Journalism which was rare in Africa then. He was number one in newspaper design and magazine layout something that in practical journalism enables copy editors to design some of the best looking newspapers and magazines on your news stands and the grocery stores today. That kind of talent and imagination shocked his professors and instructors.

He was also writing a weekly column in for one of the weekly newspapers in Kenya then, known as *"Taifa Leo"(Daily Nation)* . He wrote that column every week in Swahili. When there was a student riot at the University of Nairobi his camera captured some of the first pictures of the scenes and those pictures appeared in newspapers in East Africa then and overseas. After finishing so high academically, he received an award to

visit 14 cities in the broadcasting networks of

Europe. There he witnessed the broadcasting

and newspaper styles of a lot of European

countries. During that time he was wooed to

work for **Reuters News Agency,** one of the

Premier British news agencies as a special

correspondent. He declined to work for Reuters

then.

Then he attended the University of Minnesota,

Minneapolis, MN, USA before heading for

Iowa State University where his musical

career was launched as he would spend time

and time writing music and leading a band instead of finishing his masters' thesis.

Today he has a lot of songs on *ITunes* all over the world and his website is huberttemba.net .and his music CDs are on *Amazon.com.* He is a prolific reader, researcher and inventor.

WHY THE SACRED WILL

OF THE PEOPLE ?

The will of the people is sacred. But that will have

sometimes been abused or misused. The human race

has been created in the image of God, the creator of

all universes, the alpha and the omega, the first and

the last. Yet it is often not noticed or remembered in

our daily encounters and life. How come a man or

woman is more intelligent than a tortoise? How come

that a dolphin lives in the sea and man does not. How

come that man can make music and another mammal

cannot make music in our human ears. We hear of

birds chirping in the early morning hours, but there

has never been a Bach, Chuck Berry, Mozart or Jimi Hendrix in the animal kingdom.

The human race was created to be supreme. But some of the human race members have squandered that privilege.

So in this essay, full of investigative reporting and result of a long research, Former Fulbright Award winner HUBERT TEMBA says that the human race has a sacred will – will to choose and deny.

But that will have been betrayed by some in the past. For example, the communist leaders of China, the former USSR and Cuba usurped power to rule and try to manage people as if they were sheep or some other domestic animals.

But the universe got hold of this, although it was after waiting for too long, maybe for a few a few light years.

This did not lighten the weight of the burden on the shoulders and backs of the people from the tyrants and dictators who usurped power under the guises of helping people and actually bathing in the eat and tears of those they oppressed and lied to.

r or it does not ease the pain on the patient.

Politicians believe and practice in their minds that everybody in their electorate is sleeping or is in some kind of confusion or mental block that they cannot understand the lies of politicians.

Back to Politicians

Who lean eastward

Talking about the world that is not western, the other world's frustrations echoed in their growls and curses could once again be heard across the great walls of the entire universe.

The communist regimes crumbled. The dust left behind after the crumbling is so huge that it makes almost all victims of mass oppression visit the USA or be a part of it.

Those who oppress and cheat others with greed end up on the cross of gross punishment.

Most of the former socialist and communist leaders who fooled people for years have ended up on the crosses of condemnation and coveted revenge.

The people should not be blamed for feeling the need to reward crime with punishment, socialist and communist leaders with extreme crucifixion. The people who have a will from God to choose their own paths in life have a right to punish those who steal that right from them.

The will of the people is sacred. Hubert Temba goes to write about the experiments of African Socialism especially in Tanzania where he was born. He says that Julius Nyerere chose the wrong path in trying to force people from their established and traditional homesteads.

[16]

Renowned psychologists worth his salt will tell you that the late Nyerere was wrong in trying to change people so rapidly.

We should never let the lies of politicians and power-hungry maniacs steal the breath of life that God has all given us.

MANY THANKS

This book was first conceived in mind in 1984, and then completed in 2008.

Thanks to Julie Rose, then Foreign Student Advisor at Iowa State University, Ames, Iowa for first typing the original manuscript. Then thanks to Michael Weilland for typing another version of the manuscript in 2007.

The author finally revisited the whole manuscript himself, bearing things are they are today, in the 21st century.

He also revised it to what it looks like today. He even wrote new things relevant to the new millennium. He even injected his journalistic genius.

DEDICATION

This book is dedicated to all those who believe love will heal the world.

LOVE,

Hubert Temba.

April 19, 2008.

THE BERLIN CONFERENCE

OF 1884-1885

TO DIVIDE AFRICA

The Berlin Conference that took place in the December 1884 to February 1885 was a sharp piece of evidence on how Europeans were determined by whatever hooks and crooks to divide and rule Africa.

The conference was the agenda setting colonialism triggering point in which European governments hungrily went on a rampage of colonizing Africa. Intelligent thinking would link this kind of motivation to the strongest degree of greed. Further analysis could result in mentioning the laws of subliminal conditioning.

Whether those leading the European governments then were subliminally responding to prior programming of their minds from historically written reports and persuasions, regarding the way one has to treat an African remains something to be investigated.

But whatever the truth is, it was the truth yesterday, it is the same today, similarly tomorrow and unshakeable throughout the annals of time. The truth is and will remain that Africans have been exploited, abused, disrespected throughout time. And this is utterly unforgivable and extremely despicable...

Even when they excel in anything including inventing and changing the world for the better, Africans are ridiculed. Who ridicules them? The one who goes to church or who does not, the one who claims and has tried to portray *Jesus Christ* as being one of them and not also one of those oppressed Africans and descendants from the Middle East.

Now we have injected one piece of information that is important enough to be mentioned.

It is one of the most ridiculous ways of thinking, what was going on the mind of Cecil Rhodes, the one who has a Cecil Rhodes Scholarship named after him. And some people who have governed the USA like Bill Clinton have benefitted from this blood-shaded scholarship.

This scholarship smells of the blood sucked during colonialism on the African continent because Cecil Rhodes had the aim and notion of colonizing *Africa* from *Cape Town* to *Cairo.* By any stretch of sober imagination this is utterly despicable and condemnable.

Such a notion and passion to do an inhuman thing of such astronomical proportions was a display of pure hunger and devilish greed.

Cecil Rhodes had the mid set that supported the *Jim Crowe Laws* in the USA. Human blood, sweat and tears are weeping.

That Africa was much divided as a result of that *Berlin Conference* is something read sad and worth mourning.

That tribes would be divided by angry power hungry colony angry European colonizer is condemnable. It is bad. Anybody with clean conscience will regret and ask for repentance.

But there is so much greed and hate among some people which is also doubled with a grand canyon of ignorance and arrogance that this may not change.

When some people are used to sinning unless they break that trend of sinning they will keep on sinning. Why should so many people carry Bibles and still practice the opposite?

Analysts, historians and observers have indicated that if there is doubt or any marking of forgiveness underlined in any book that mentions

God, this kind of dividing people and ruling them is and should all the time remain unforgivable.

The **Bible** and any sermons about forgiveness do not carry water in this kind of treating of **Africans** throughout the span of time, one renowned journalist and columnist has remarked...

There is no book, there is no creation by a human being, that lays down the rules of free will and freedom from slavery and freedom from being exploited that will stand the scorching rays of the sun when the Son of Love and True Justice is Shining.

It is a pity that one human race will love and hunger to steal from another. It is primitive and cannibalistic.

The animals in Kenya would like to slaughter and eat each other.

The ***Berlin Conference*** attendees were doing something not dissimilar from the way animals behave. Take anything precious from another, including and not limited to raping their women. And they did.

Look at one of the most heinous crimes of the ***Berlin Conference*** of the 1880s. The aftermath of that conference include the division of the ***Masai*** Tribe and other tribes into two or three political states on the African continent.

There are ***Masai*** tribesmen in Kenya who have cousins and nephews and other relatives in neighboring countries who wonder even today why they cannot move freely from one place to another without being asked for passports and other documents.

Remember when a family is not divided and you come over here or meet over there to reschedule the way they should move is wrong and unforgivable.

The Europeans in the ***Berlin Conference*** of the 1880s did the same thing…dividing a whole race.

If you go back to the annals of history you will notice a trend of abuse and colonization by the European race. Despicable is the word and unforgivable and punishable are the words which logically follow. Crime and what deserves to follow is disciplining and punishment. "Spanking." "Spare the rod, spoil the child."

And they are still dividing races as we speak. Greed is a very bad evil. There are a lot of people divided because of the criminality of the Berlin Conference.

There are a lot of people who are fighting because of the reverberations of the *Berlin Conference* that met to unite and discuss how to rapture Africa. That is unforgivable. Still they are divided because of the *Berlin Conference*. Hunger and Greed was the key of the *Berlin Conference*. Greed has been known to be very deep in evil. So is selfishness and prejudice. All these worms can fill a box of evil eruptions.

To have a mindset that will let one nation or government that will endorse going to another country to steal slaves for their benefits is questionable. To have a mindset that favors exploitation and colonialism is something very unfavorable. For the way man and woman were created, it was in the sweet and beautiful image of God.

The image of God is perfect and beautiful. That the image of God is in all of creation is something not debatable. This is the final truth.

The beauty and mightiness of God is nothing to debate about. It is as ethereal as the smell of air without aromas.

But there are people who have been stuck in the primitive thinking of taking advantage of others, exploiting them. Most of those people participated in the Berlin Conference of the 1880s that divided and

29

demarcated Africa with its people, opening the

threshold to the homestead of colonialism.

As I stand here, a man who was helped by a

Jewish man, who told me in the elevator things that

are good about God, and that God has done certain

things to me, I have to report:

CHAPTER ONE:

Introduction:

Communication for Development

In the 1960s, many countries of the Third

World were beginning to look for unorthodox

solutions to the educational problem they had inherited.

The expansion of schools, within the limits imposed by finance and by the supply of teachers, could not keep pace with the demand for education, even within a generation or more.

The number of children seeking to enter primary school was dwarfed by the number of adults who never went to school, or who did not complete their school courses.

Most of these countries were hindered by ignorance, disease and poverty. These problems tend to be interrelated. In the rural areas of these countries, a majority of the populations lived a marginal existence in low productivity agricultural work.

Most governments wanted their masses of rural poor to "modernize," become more productive, eat better, get basic education, produce fewer children, have better health. Because of the level of literacy of the masses, governments found it easier to reach them through radio.

To effect changes, governments found it imperative to persuade the masses. Such communication was important because the people ought to know the goals and programs of development (Jamison and MaAnany, 1978).

There was the massive problem of trying to awaken the bulk of the people to new ideas and to the potentialities of new techniques. Unless the masses of the people were exposed to new ways of thinking and led to adopt new attitudes, there could be little hope of any steady progress toward economic development, social modernization, and political maturity (Pye, 1963, p. 13).

Development communication which relied much on persuasion was often used to reinforce existing values and behavior patterns or to encourage new behaviors.

The central governments made sure that the media were not used for criticizing the messages which the governments wanted the masses to receive. In the People's Republic of China, it was used to reinforce communism, by telling the people how bad the previous regime was, or how evil capitalism was, so the government was seen in good light.

In Tanzania and other Third World countries, persuasion was used in such a way that the government and party in control were seen as benefactors of the people. They were seen as the vehicles of salvation for the masses.

New behaviors may have been introduced to the people by persuasion, depending on the road needed to be taken. New policies were introduced, new development plans were made.

Whether or not the policies and development plans were accepted by the people depends on how they are communicated to the masses in the presence of old behaviors and attitudes.

In most Third World countries the governments held a lot of power in their hands. They used some of this power to decide which development directions their people will take. Many of these countries persuaded the masses to take certain development directions.

Most Third World countries were one-party states. The presence of single parties did not allow any opposition to the political system or the path of development that the government had decided to follow.

THE MEANING OF COMMUNICATION

There are many definitions of ***communication.*** One of the broadest defines it as an ***information-sharing activity.*** An extended definition of communication as a process and the factors central to that process is of value. ***Communication*** is a dynamic process in which man can consciously or unconsciously affects the cognitions of another through materials or agencies used in symbolic ways.

From the communicator's point of view, it is a process by which he seeks to influence the cognitions of another in desired ways through the use of symbols. From the receiver's point of view, it is a process by which he perceives, interprets, and responds in some way to a stimulus provided by a source (Andersen, 1972, p. 4).

The process of communication is in operation all the time and certain segments of the process may represent longer periods of time than others (American Association of Agricultural College Editors, 1970, p. 3).

SOURCE is anyone, any group, or even an institution that can initiate a message.

RECEIVER is the individual who perceives a "message" in a channel. While he is often regarded as the passive partner, he actually is not at all passive. Whereas a source can only encode a message and put it into the channel, the receiver must act to extract the message from the channel, and give meaning to the stimuli.

MESSAGE is the constellation of the stimuli that the source actually places in the channel(s). It is only a set of physical stimuli which exist in the channel.

CHANNEL is the medium in which the message exists. Anything that can affect the sensory mechanisms, i.e. the senses of sight, hearing, touch, or smell, can be used as a communication medium.

PERSUASION

Brembeck and Howell (1952) consider persuasion as "the conscious attempt to modify thought and action by manipulating the motives of men toward predetermined ends."

Thayer (1961) sees persuasion as "a conscious effort made by people to affect other people's behavior in a specific circumstance or at a specific time." Wright and Warner (1962) consider persuasion as "an active attempt to influence people to action or belief by an overt appeal to reason or emotion."

Minick (1957) prefers a definition of persuasion as "discourse, written or oral, that is designed to stimulate action by employing all of the factors that determine human behavior." Blau and Scott (1962) note that "in persuasion, on person lets the arguments of another person influence his decisions or actions."

Wilson and Arnold (1964) similarly emphasize the stimuli involved as a basis for defining persuasion.

For Eisenson, Auer and Irwin (1963), *"persuasion in public address is defined as the process of securing acceptance of an idea, or an action, by connecting it favorably with the listener's attitudes, beliefs, and desires."*

In a different vein, Johnson (1956) sees persuasion as primarily and ability: *"there is a particular art, the art of persuasion, that has as its major purpose the control of the effects that words shall have."*

[39]

FUNCTIONS OF

PERSUASION

Persuasion spreads new information and ideas. The mere possession of new information is not sufficient to cause people to transmit it, but when people are motivated to communicate material which may be of value to the receiver; it is persuasion (Andersen, 1972, p. 220).

Persuasion supplies a way for decisions to be reached and for changes to be made or accepted. Persuasion serves as means of getting things done – new programs, new policies, and new approaches can be offered and accepted or rejected.

The persuasion process makes influencing the wills of a society possible. Those who influence against their wills use persuasion. A society that loves socialism or communism can be caught on the limb using propaganda and persuasion to people's minds and habits.

During the cold war and during famed propaganda periods about the former Soviet Union propaganda was as rampant as termites eating a hill. It was so rampant that there was a bad relationship between the west and the east. And in the midst of all those cold wars of the past, lots of people's lives were lost.

Decision-making power rested on the chest of Mao Tse Tung (Communist leader of Red China, and no wonder China is very famous for her lead and the abuse of human rights), on the chest of the Soviet Communist practitioners, Marx, Stalin and Lenin until the walls came tumbling down in the early 1980s. Evil destroys itself in its own time.

Many of these leaders of socialism and communism were almost if not completely fanatic at using force, or just using the mass media however they wished to persuade the masses.

Persuasion was involved in any decision-making process, but how it is used, who uses it, and to whom the effort is directed, varies. Every dictator was dependent upon others for information and advice, which makes him subject to persuasion.

Enforcement always involved some degree of persuasion.

During the times when socialism and communism was breathing with a lot of vigor, persuasion supplied a way for decisions to be reached and for changes to be made or accepted. Persuasion served as means of getting things done – new programs, new policies, and new approaches can be offered and accepted or rejected.

Communicators believed that a society must have a means of reaching and implementing decisions. But there was the risk that decision-making power could be vested in one man, in a select group, or theoretically, in everyone.

But the danger of greed taking over and have one person or one group that raped the wills and freedoms of the people was very possible and easy.

Because of the easiness in usurping power, politicians have cheated wearing masquerades. Most politicians wear masks and cheat the masses of the people.

There is a tendency by many politicians to go against the wills of the people by twisting a lie here and but distorting a truth there in order to get into power for as long as possible.

Many politicians suffer from the vulnerability to the evils of corruption, cheating here, accepting lobbyists' money there, and stealing peoples' money over there.

The sins that politicians fall into are almost similar universally. It is based on the love for self and love for money or falling into the bear traps of sex and scandal over here until they are caught in a sex or drug sting operation.

But the watchdogs in the political spheres of the third world are not skilled or disciplined to sniff like the dogs in western countries.

That may explain why people like *Mobutu Tsetse Tseko* of Zaire, or *Hastings Banda* of Malawi, or *Robert Mugabwe* if Zimbabwe got away with it for so long.

But even the watchdog system of the west has its own failings.

The point this author is trying to make here is that politicians are tempted to or do anything to grasp power. Many politicians are shrouded in the mask of pretending and trying to fulfill their thirst for power, and of course the amassing of money like corporate chief executive officers. This is an ultimate example of human greed. observers and sympathizers have expressed concerns.

Greed was the reason for the Berlin Conference of the 1880s that displaced many tribes of Africa. Greed was the reason why Nyerere's father was selected by the hungry Germans to be a chief of the Zanaki people, a people who did not have a chief at all.

Fanatics of socialism and communism, who sometimes called themselves *"Cadres"* in Tanzania thought those decisions in mass persuasion should have been implemented through force, through general acceptance, or through persuasion.

Persuasion was involved in many decision-making processes, but how it was used, who used it, and to whom the effort was directed, varied.

Every dictator was so dependent upon others for information and advice, which makes him subject to persuasion. Enforcement always involved some degree of persuasion.

Summary

Political persuasion was an important part of development communication. When political persuasion was used, it was for the promotion of Development Goals in different contexts of Third World countries. These goals included:

(1) *Helping to increase people's participation in their own education and development;*

(2) *Mobilization of large masses of people in study campaigns;*

(3) *Improvement of instructional quality and learning;*

> *(4)   Improving health, agricultural and nutritional practices through improved information and education;*
>
> *(5)   Improving organization and administration through better one-way and two-way communication (McAnany and Mayo, 1980, p. 69).*

This study looked at communication in development. It looked at how governments and political parties link their political messages to the development messages and how they are credited with the benefits of the message.

The Tanzanian *ujamaa* village settlement experiment was taken as an example of the Third World countries. The mass media and interpersonal communication were both used in political persuasion in the Tanzania *ujamaa* experiment.

Also projects in four countries were compared to the *ujamaa* experiment and the important role of persuasion is underscored.

The communication campaigns were examined in their political environments. Different levels of politicization were looked at in the countries. The countries were Tunisia, Kenya and Trinidad and Tobago.

CHAPTER TWO:

POLITICAL PERSUASION

LITERATURE REVIEW

A look at the literature on persuasion showed that in the 1940s and 1950s persuasion was used mainly in propaganda campaigns and public relations work, especially in political elections.

In the 20th century, radio s became a vital medium of persuasion (Brembeck and Howell, 1964, p. 398). The use of political persuasion together with coercion and education had been very helpful in development in Third World countries.

Most of this happened starting in the 1960s when these countries attained their independence. Radio had thus been used as a tool of propaganda and as an important medium of development communication.

Persuasive

Communication and

Development

Beginning in the 1940s, political persuasion mainly involved propaganda and public relations campaigns. Most studies have been done on these types of campaigns and little on political persuasion.

Inkeles (in Lazafeld and Stanton, 1949, pp. 223-293), made a report of survey on broadcasting in the USSR, covering program content and audience analysis.

He noted that broadcasting was accomplished principally through a network of wired loudspeakers.

The audience could receive only approved programs; and wired programs could be confined to the desired audience.

As far as public relations campaigns were concerned, Mott (1944, pp. 348-367) made an investigation in years of U.S. presidential elections from 1792 to 1944. He found no correlation of any significance between newspaper and the outcome of the presidential campaigns.

Janowitz (1944, pp. 84-92) analyzed the content of 63 radio speeches of Gerald L.E. Smith(then candidate for the U.S. Senate) from December 14, 1941 to November 15, 1942. He classified Smith's persuasion under fourteen "Major Radio Propaganda Themes" and tabulated their relative frequencies.

Two survey studies during U.S. elections in the 1940s attempted to measure the extent of mass media influence on voters (Lazarsfeld et al., 1948; Berelson et al., 1954).

These sociologists concluded that few voters were converted and that interpersonal influence outweighed any media impact.

Social psychologists who examined political communication in the 1950s and 1960s emphasized the partisan nature of information processing (especially selective exposure to congruent messages), the resistance to attitudinal change, and the importance of reinforcement of predispositions (Sears and Freedman, 1967; McGuire, 1969; Weiss, 1969; Sears and Whitney, 1973).

Persuasive communication had been used together with coercion and education in development communication.

Persuasive communication in the guise of development could be exemplified by the "group planning of births" at the village level in the People's Republic of China, where the villagers decide how many babies they should each have and who should have them.

Most nations in the past had implicitly defined development in terms of what government does to (and for) the people.

Decisions about needed development were made by the national government in the capital city and then through development programs that were carried out by government employees who contacted the public (at the operational level) in order to inform and persuade them to change some aspect of their behavior.

This top-to-bottom approach to development implied a one-way role for communication: the sources were government officials seeking to inform and persuade a mass audience of receivers.

In recent years, several nations (examples the People's Republic of China, Tanzania, the Republic of Korea, and Taiwan) have recognized the importance of self-development at the village and urban neighborhood level.

In this approach, some type of small group at the local level (mothers' clubs in Korea, farmers' associations in Taiwan, radio listening clubs in Tanzania, and communes and work brigades in China) took primary responsibility (1) for deciding exactly what type of development was most needed in their village or neighborhood, (2) for planning how to achieve this development goal, (3) for obtaining whatever government or nongovernmental resources may be necessary, and (4) for carrying out their own development activities.

The Trinidad and Tobago Breastfeeding Campaign, conceived in 1974, involved messages that were carried by radio and television and also carried by newspapers, posters and handbills.

The persuasive campaign was managed by media professionals who coordinated nine television programs and a series of daily five-minute radio broadcasts (Leslie, 1977, pp. 4-6)

Beginning in 1969 in India, radio spots were used together with press inserts, billboards, wall paintings, short black-and-white films, special editions of tabloid newspapers, calendars, booklets, and comic books to determine the effectiveness of a mixed-media campaign in raising levels of awareness and understanding about weaning and pregnancy among rural, largely illiterate populations (Parlato, 1973; Moss, 1978, p. 11).

In Tunisia, radio and interpersonal communication were used beginning 1975 to test the effectiveness of combining existing face-to-face education with inexpensive radio nutrition education.

Radio was selected as the medium for this campaign because it seemed the best means of reaching the largest number of rural mothers.

The most clearly demonstrable success of the program had been the adoption of mass communication as an ongoing nutrition-education strategy by the Tunisian National Institute of Nutrition (Agence de Cooperation Culturelle et Technique, La Vulgarisation Agricole en Tunisie, Direct, June 1974, pp. 32-33).

In Tanzania, beginning in 1971, radios, cassette recorders, printed materials, interpersonal communication, flipcharts, and posters were used to provide villagers with basic information on disease control, and the relationship between environment and health.

The "Man is Health" project was a large-scale campaign aimed primarily at education villagers on the symptoms, prevalence, and origins of five controllable widespread diseases.

An estimated two million Tanzanian adults, twice the number officials had hoped to reach, participated in the "Man is Health" project. The overall participation rate of those who attended from the beginning was 63 percent (Hall and Dodds, 1974; Grenholm, 1974).

In September of 1960, Fidel Castro told the UN General Assembly that Cuba planned to "launch an all-out offensive against illiteracy….Within a few months, Cuba will be the first country in the Americas to be able to claim that it has not a single illiterate."

The Cuban literacy project was officially launched on New Year's Eve of the same year and Castro called on the Army of Education to organize just as the National Militia had done.

As a mass communication model, the Cuban literacy campaign must be viewed as a whole, because the political aspect was intertwined tightly with the educational effort (hall, 1978).

The conscious political exercise enhanced the effectiveness of the literacy training; in which reading and writing were taught to the quarter of the Cuban population denied such instruction under the pre-revolutionary regime. Reciprocally, the spread of literacy skills quickened people's responses to the call for political commitment.

The Cuban literacy campaign was a political commitment. The campaign resembled other Cuban programs in its emphasis upon citizen participation as a goal in itself. An editorial in *GRAMMA,* the government newspaper, on the sixth anniversary of the Cuban Revolution, said of the "new man" emerging:

This conception (of the new man) obliges the revolution to develop plans involving increased participation by the masses in the execution of diverse tasks .... The masses will daily have to Increase their participation in social tasks, paying more and more attention to the management and direction of these activities.

The literacy campaign was born of a spirit of development in which progress and change emerge when more and more people act in the collective, as opposed to the individual, interest. These activities "wordlessly, but dramatically, teach the lessons of development and under development" (Fagan, 1969).

Cuba set up a *National Literacy Commission* including representatives of the Ministry of Education, the Ministry of the Armed Forces, and mass organizations of workers, teachers, students, and others.

At the heart of the crusade to teach 979,000 illiterates were more than 270,000 literacy workers from among at least four different groups:

People's Instructors — 120,000 adult volunteers who taught largely in cities and towns;

Conrado Benitez brigadistas — around 100,000 young volunteers, mostly students, who in April 1961 began living and teaching in rural areas;

School teacher brigadistas — 37,772 regular school teachers who served primarily as specialists and supervisors during the campaign, working on it fulltime after April 1961; and "Patria o Murte" brigadistas — around 13,016 urban workers who taught in rural areas while fellow workers filled in for them at their city jobs.

Although radio was not used to teach literacy in Cuba, it served well to "persuade the illiterate population to enroll, encourage widespread public support and attract volunteers and support, and spread technical aspects of the campaign" (*UNESCO,* 1965).

From the time the campaign was three months old, the National Radio began broadcasting about fifteen spot announcements a day in support of the campaign. People wrote songs, jingles, and at least on whole book of poetry to celebrate the literacy drive.

Wu Chieh-ping begins an article in *The Partisan Review* on health and medical work with these words: "T mass line 'from the masses to the masses' is the fundamental line guiding all the work of our party. So it is with the health work" (1975). Characterized briefly, medical and health work in the **People's Republic of China** gave priority to prevention and rural health measures, promoting the full involvement of peasants and workers in their own health care. Wu continues:

The principle of 'putting prevention first' therefore can be put into practice only by launching mass movements to give scope to the masses' enthusiasm politically and ideologically, constantly increasing their knowledge concerning science and hygiene and carrying out regular mass activities in health work.

The idea of integrating health work into the mass-based organization appeared to have evolved out of experience in those regions that were won before the final victory of Communist forces in 1949, what had become periodic health campaigns dates from the Korean War.

Many Chinese were shown films of American pilots confessing to the use of bacteriological weapons in Korea, and the basics of germ theory were quickly brought home to millions.

There was propaganda that American actions in Korea as well as Japanese's attempted to spread plague during World War II. This kind of persuasion, this kind of propaganda aroused deep pain, deep frustration, indignation and the need to revenge by Chinese people everywhere "and prompted the masses to extend aid to the government in anti-epidemic work and health work" (Fu, 1959).

Mass health movements swept China several times a year, with most campaigns timed to precede national holidays.

Movements might have focused on indoor and outdoor sanitation, on prevention and treatment of seasonal diseases, on improvement of working conditions, or on popularization of hygienic habits and physical checkups.

As Wu Chieng-ping put it, "Mass participation in medical and health work has proved that this work cannot possibly be done well without extensively mobilizing the masses and earnestly pooling their wisdom and drawing on their experience."

Demonstrating the high value they placed on communication, the Chinese began early to set up networks of local transmitters and public address and loudspeaker systems throughout the country (Schutman, 1969). In 1965, the central government spelled out three broad goals for the continuing expansion of rural broadcasting:

- *Each hsien (country) was to have one broadcasting station to be financed entirely by the central government.*
- *Each commune and production brigade was to be allowed to have its own broadcasting station for which the commune brigade could accord to its needs, receive partial subsidy from the central government.*
- *Any household in the village was to be permitted to have a radio-speaker for which an installment fee of four dollars was to be charged (Lee, 1972).*

Besides relying on radio coverage, nearly all Chinese campaigns made wide use of discussion groups or forums. The groups received from the government written materials relation to the campaign, and local party cadres usually supplied the discussion leaders.

Group sessions stimulated a two-way information flow between cadre members and group participants. Films, slide shows, and opera were also employed in campaign efforts.

In addition, large-character wall posters made by workers, students, and peasants were sometimes used to convey the messages of the campaigns.

It should be noted that radio forums were aimed at relatively small numbers of listening groups over an extended period of time. Examples were the Indian radio rural forums (UNSECO, 1956), and Ghana's village forums (Coleman, Opeku, and Abell, 1968).

Mass campaigns were meant to mobilize large numbers of people for a relatively short time. Mass campaigns often relied on political mobilization as a base for stimulation widespread reflection and action on educational or health concerns. The communicating strategy stressed mass media, including broadcast, print, billboards, and popular theater (Hall, 1978).

No matter how attractive a radio strategy might have been for achieving certain goals, if the political leadership failed to support the goals and their achievement, then a project would have difficulty succeeding (McAnany and Jamison, 1978).

Some of the goals took a strong national determination to carry out because they were complicated and costly to solve.

The success of the radio campaign in Tanzania was partly explained by the national commitment that the government had to be the enforcer of mobilization of the people for their own development, and the concomitant investment of resources in rural services.

Other projects failed or only managed to survive at a low level because there was no more than an oral commitment to the proposed goals.

A leader who had both vision and the political skill to win backing and get others to cooperate with him could have made a major difference in success or failure of mass media projects.

Colombia's radio school project, ACPO *(Popular Cultural Action),* owed a great deal of its success to its founder and leader for thirty years, Father Salcedo. **Radio Santa Maria** in the Dominican Republic (White, 1977a) also could partly attribute its success to a dynamic leader.

A common problem for radio projects was that although government officials agreed that the idea was a good one, it had often come from an external technical-assistance agency and there was no leader to make it work locally.

An added problem was that trained leadership talent in low-income countries was often in short supply and there was a quick turnover of these people in their jobs as they moved up the career ladder

(McAnany and Jamison, 1978).

In 1973, the Philippines faced an agricultural

crisis. Drought, typhoon, floods, and plant disease

cut rise production in half.

The fragile Filipino national economy could not

tolerate importing the amounts of rice needed to

compensate for this loss in production.

Instead, the Philippines launched a national

self-help program, a rice-growing campaign that the

country would come to know as *Masagana 99*

(Merrick, 1981).

The planners who designed the campaign were

inspired by the charismatic energies of the Minister of

Agriculture, Arturo Tanco.

Upon a presidential order in 1973, the Central Bank of the Philippines organized a credit system to provide loans without collateral to poor farmers.

Credit was available only to farmers cultivating relatively small portions of land, and only to those who promised to participate in the *Masagana 99* program.

Radio was the most persuasive communication medium used to mobilize and educate the Filipino farmers.

In this campaign, the role played by the government was evident – the inspiration given by the Minister of Agriculture, Arturo Tanco, and the presidential order of 1973 which directed the Central bank of the Philippines to organize a credit system to provide loans without collateral to poor farmers.

By 1976, the *Masagana 99* campaign had transformed the Philippines from a rice-importing to a rice-exporting nation.

Traditionally, in the Philippines, radio had been used to reach farms scattered over the country's many islands. So, the government leadership harnessed an array of communications strategies to do the task of reaching the archipelago's 7,000 islands during the *Masagana 99* campaign.

These strategies included instructional radio broadcasts, radio jingles, occasional flags, car stickers, and campaign logos (Maverick, 1981.)

In the Philippines, starting in 1975, radio and limited interpersonal communication were used to test the effectiveness of modern marketing and advertising techniques in changing behavior, attitudes and knowledge related to the nutrition and health of infants (Manoff, et al., 1977).

CONCLUSION

Most Third World countries adopted a mass communication model close or similar to the communist model. The communist theory of mass communication is emphatic on the possible negative effects of some messages and opposition messages were simply banned.

Terror assures that only the approved ideas will flow to the public, without tolerance of even slight deviations.

The communist propaganda rulebook required that the agitator always exhort to specific actions rather than simply advocate attitudes.

The communists thought of using the mass media to produce character logical change (Pool, 1963, pp. 238-239).

In communist countries, person-to-person communication was known as "oral agitation." If one took into account the fact that this was a communist scheme of communication that involved literally millions of communicators and huge segments of the Chinese population, for instance, this was definitely a form of mass communication and without doubt mass persuasion.

Propagandists were established by the Central Committee of the Chinese Communist Party on January 1, 1951.

These propagandists carried on a variety of activities among the masses, such as interviewing, passing on information, reading newspapers (in newspaper reading groups), monitoring broadcasts, preparing posters, editing wall newspapers or black board newspapers, leading discussion meetings, etc.

Many of the propagandists used personal conversation as their form of carrying out their propaganda mission.

They were supposed to be constantly at work among people in the homes, quarters, and daily activities and to seize every opportunity to carry on propaganda, even at meal time (Yu, 1964, p. 288)

Persuasive communications played a conspicuous part in the total policy of the Chinese Communist regime.

The rulers in Peking had always depended upon hypnotic indoctrination and stirring propaganda to mobilize the minds and effort of the population, to carry out tasks of the party leadership, and to facilitate control of the nation. Persuasive communications were indispensable political tools in all communist and totalitarian societies.

Many of Peking's principles of propaganda and techniques of persuasion were obviously borrowed from or inspired by the Soviet Union.

But the Bolshevik attempt to remold the thinking of the Russian population (not just party members and government cares) in the post-1917 era

did not warrant comparison with the Chinese

Communist performance in intensity, scope and skill

(Yu, 1963, p. 259).

In the developing nations, it was the approach

to propaganda and politics which had been the most

effective part of Bolshevik doctrine.

Words in the media alone did not effectively

change people.

The norm is that it takes a combination of the

media and direct personal contact to move people to

action.

It is only through participation in action that

deeply held attitudes are changed. It is only through

the change of the thinking (conscious mind and the

continuous thinking of similar thoughts for a certain amount of time that peoples' characters will change.

You can't just force people from one place to another or from one way of thinking to another without working on their minds. Psychologists, philosophers and thinkers will agree with this.

But that is why propaganda or the cold war was sending messages from left or right. Communist China under Mao Tse Tung sent out messages which were not true about the western capitalistic culture, then presented as being evil in the eyes of the eastern socialist and communist oriented worlds.

Propaganda was rampant. It would feed the minds of the citizens with a lot of information stressing that the west was bad. The west was capitalistic. And the west was bad because capitalism was bad.

If there was no definition of the west with the adjective of being capitalistic, things would have been different. But socialist and communism practitioners harbored their propaganda and most of their information dissipation telling or informing their masses that the west was bad because the west was practicing capitalism and that since capitalism was bad, therefore the west was bad and socialism and communism were the saviors of the masses.

The propaganda was so much repeated even forced on people's throats that it became more or so of a tyranny. Socialism and communism societies were tyrannically run operations by dictators. Now

China is sending out toys to kids to the world which have lead in them. Is that what you get from communism for many years?

The Soviet Union is not defunct, and Ukraine which is one of the largest former USSR member states was not even admitted to NATO when she asked to, lately, given that this book is being completed in early 2008. The questionability of this goes beyond any commonsense.

If it is tit for tat or if it is Russia then there should be Ukraine in NATO. African countries should also belong to NATO. Japan and Hong Kong and Mexico should belong to NATO too. To subliminally derail the free thinking of people can be viewed or termed as despicable.

That is why advertising works so well by telling the same lie over and over again. Many psychologists and experts on the science of mind will agree with me here.

By action, however, these can be changed, even down to changing the basic personality of man (Pool, 1963, pp. 240-241).

It is worth mentioning again that persuasion takes place in many forms. It is not necessary that those participating in it acknowledge that they are the subjects of persuasion.

It should be stressed that the relationship between persuasion and communication is that persuasion is always conscious activity. Gerald Miller and Michael Burgoon (1973) advocate this position. While they would not deny that people can unintentionally influence, their perspective implies that it is impossible to unintentionally persuade.

A second condition of persuasion is the perception of threat to one's goals. The threat need not be explicit – merely sufficient in the eyes of one individual to warrant an attempt to change the behavior of the other(s).

A third difference between persuasion and communication involves self-concept. Self-concept plays a much more central role in interpersonal persuasion than it does in communication.

The suggestion that one should change always implies some level of inadequacy on the part of the one being persuaded.

Also, persuaders do not seek to change the behavior of others unless such a change has implications for their own self-concepts (Beardon, 1981, p. 24).

In the preceding examples where persuasion took place, it was implicit if not explicit in many cases.

There were conscious attempts to change the behaviors of the target audiences. The information was tailored for such ends.

The goals of persuasion were defined by the ruling bodies. The communication strategies (whatever name they are given were laid down.) The plans were thus implemented.

Development communication was mostly persuasion because of the conscious attempt to change the behavior of the masses from one style of living to another.

The mere suggestion that one should change implies some inadequacy on the part of those who are the objects of persuasion.

In the Third World countries, the inadequacy was often in literacy, health standards, life expectancies, feeding practices, and other aspects of life.

CHAPTER THREE:

BACKGROUND TO THE

UJAMAA (FAMILYHOOD)

EXPERIMENT

The Tanzanian ***ujamaa*** (family hood)

villagization movement, which began in 1967, has

been a unique experiment that subtly used the

persuasive powers of the media aided by coercion and

education to achieve its goals. The purpose of this

study is to look at the role political persuasion played

in the Tanzanian ***ujamaa*** villagization movement.

McHenry (1979) has said that one of the most

important efforts to initiate a form of socialist change

in rural areas was the struggle to implement ***ujamaa***
village policy in Tanzania. The writer McHenry
further claimed that the ***ujamaa*** village policy was the
type of African socialism.

African socialism had been an important
ideological concept among many African elites. This
concept existed in minds of these elites whether they
got their education from the USA, Cuba, China, the
Soviet Union, and Britain or even from their home
countries' higher institutions of learning.

This kind of socialism existed, mushroomed,
grew and overflowed in the minds of the elites.

But when that kind of mentally grown type of
socialism came to the time of implementation, these

elites resorted to propaganda, persuasion, force and even ridicule or sacrilege.

To force someone to leave the place of their ancestors because of some socialistic concept that mushroomed in the minds of a few elites is tantamount to sacrilege and a humiliation cum breach of human rights.

Leaders in a number of African countries have expounded theories and programs for socialism, African style (Friedland and Rosberg, 1964).

But how they have mobilized their masses to follow the ideologies they have expounded is indeed not free from persuasion, force or education.

However, it is not the purpose of this study to go into each and every experiment of socialism and see how they have used mass media.

The situation in Tanzania prior to the *ujamaa* village policy was one of underdevelopment. It included:

1. *A large rural population. In 1967 over 11 million people, 94 percent of the total population, lived in rural areas (Tanzania, Quarterly Statistical Bulletin, 26, 1 (June 1975): sec. 1).*

2. *A scattered pattern of rural settlement. It was estimated in 1965 that 86.3 percent of the total or 91 percent of the rural population live in scattered homesteads –*

[94]

outside villages or urban areas (Georgulas, 1967, p. 28).

3. *A relatively rapid drift of population to the towns. Between 1957 and 1967, urban areas had experienced an average growth rate of about 6.4 percent per year, more than twice that of the country as a whole (Jensen and Mkama, 1968, p. 77).*

4. *The percentage of subsistence agriculture as the dominant form of rural production. Between 1961, the year of independence, and 1967, the subsistence share of agricultural production declined only from 59 percent to 55.1 percent (Tanzania,*

Statistical Abstract, 1968, pp. 144- 145;

1972, p. 165).

5. *A low level of technology employed in agriculture. The hoe remained the primary tool of the agricultural production.*

6. *<u>A falling per capita income from agriculture</u>. The gross domestic product per capita (GDP/capita) from agriculture in 1961 was Shs. 242; in 1967 it was Shs. 239 (Tanzania, Statistical Abstract, 1966, pp. 24 and 143; 1970, pp. 44 and 165).*

7. *<u>Significant and growing inequalities in the distribution of income</u>. The decline in per capita income of those in the agricultural*

sector was accompanied by a rise in income of those outside that sector. As a result, the total GDP/capita rose from Shs. 411 (about $59) in 1961 to Shs. 568 (about $81) in 1967. There was also wide variation in the distribution of income among districts.

8. *<u>Limited services available to the people</u>. In 1967, there were on 373 doctors in the country, or one for every 31, 842 people (Tanzania, Statistical Abstract, 1970, p. 195). Only about 24 percent of children, 5 to 14 years old, were in primary schools (Dgero and Henin, 1970). In both cases, there was a significant bias in the*

distribution of services favoring urban areas.

9. *A growing reliance on foreign assistance.*

The proportion of the total development budget in the form of loans and grants from external sources rose from 35.3 percent in 1963-64 to 38.4 percent in 1964-65, declined to 36.3 percent in 1965-66, and rose again to 43.2 percent in 1966-67 (Tanzania, Statistical Abstract, 1970, p. 195). This meant a reduction in the freedom to decide the nature of development and an increase in indebtedness and dependence.

10.   *An increase in the centralization of authority.* Despite major efforts at increasing popular participation through village development committees (VDCs) and district councils, there was a tendency toward oligarchy and authoritarian rule (Pratt, 1976, p. 257).

11.   *A commitment by political leaders to building a socialist society.* Early in 1967, the President prepared, and the party approved, the Arusha Declaration, which explicitly directed the country's efforts toward building a socialist society (Nyerere, 1968a, p. 231-250).

Previous Attempts To force/move People ("peasants") from one village To another

Moving people into villages was sought during the period of colonial rule through the concentration policy and during the early years of independence through the village settlement scheme. During those years, efforts to induce people to work together encouraging cooperative societies and initiating widely diverse projects requiring joint labor (McHenry, 1979, p.14).

Many explanations have been offered to account for the scattered nature of the rural population noted in the preceding paragraphs.

The one frequently used is that prior to colonization, people lived in defensive communities (Fairbairn, 1943-44). The people in them were dispersed for various reasons, including the suppression by tribal wars, the devastation caused by the demands upon villages for porters during World War I, and the desire of individuals to free themselves from governmental control and exactions (Fairbairn and Maclean, 1929).

Settlement was supposed to help to solve a number of problems. During the early years of British colonial rule, tsetse flies had spread over much of the territory and had become a major threat to man and his animals.

The flies carried sleeping sickness, which broke out in a series of epidemics. The major outbreaks between 1922 and 1954 were four (Pated, 1962).

An obvious solution to the problem was to separate man from the flies. A major outbreak in Uganda at the turn of the century was controlled by the massive movement of population.

The *Maswa* outbreak in 1922 also was dealt with by moving people into fly-free areas (Apted, 1962), but such areas were not large enough to accommodate the affected population in the Western Province. As a result, the policy of establishing concentrations was initiated.

The first sleeping-sickness officer, C.F.M. Swynnerton, defined a concentration as a group of people *"sufficiently closely scattered to bring about and maintain automatically, with the aid of their animals, a country practically devoid of visible brush"* (Swynnerton, 1924).

The village settlement policy, however, grew out of dissatisfaction with the slow rate of general development in rural areas. In an attempt to increase rural production, the British undertook a massive mechanical farming effort in the late 1940s which

104

became known as the groundnut scheme (Wood, 1950).

So many problems arose that the project turned out to be one of the greatest failures in colonial development history.

Nyerere, in his inaugural address as President of Tanzania in 1962, argued that unless people move into villages,

> *We shall not be able to provide ourselves with the things we shall not be able to use tractors; we shall not be able to provide schools for our children; we shall not be able to provide schools for our children; we shall not be able to build hospitals, or have clean drinking water; it will be quite impossible to start*

*small village industries; and
instead we shall have to go
on depending on the towns
for all our requirements;
and even if we had a
plentiful supply of electric
power we should never be
able to connect it to each
isolated homestead.... If
we do not start living in
proper village communities
then all our attempts to
develop the country will be
just so much wasted effort
(Nyerere, 1966, p. 184).*

Nyerere stressed the gradual concentration of

the population in villages in inhabited areas. His

objective was to make it possible for services such as

health, education, communications, and water to be

provided at moderate cost, inasmuch as "they are

essential prerequisites to higher production, better

living and increased capital accumulation for the general economic development of the country" (Tanganyika Rural Settlement Commission, Vice President's Office, n.d. (1964), p. 1).

Planning for implementation of the two policies differed considerably. In the case of the concentrations, it centered primarily on the movement of people; in the case of the village settlements, it concerned mainly the development of the village after the movement.

Fairbairn has described planning for concentrations, once sleeping sickness was found, in terms of the following steps:

> *1. The number of people who would have to move would be determined.*

[106]

2. *The people affected would be asked to suggest possible sites for the village.*

3. *A sleeping-sickness surveyor with the help of elders would locate the most suitable area*

4. *The choice would be put before the chief and the people affected agree with the site or an alternative one.*

5. *Boundaries would be marked, enclosing eight acres per family.*

6. *Arrangements would be made for transportation of peasants and their possessions (Fairbairn, 1943-44, pp. 18-19).*

The cost of the concentration policy was much less than of the village settlement scheme.

Mechanism for Gaining Popular Compliance

Different types of recruitment campaigns were conducted to induce the target populations to move into concentrations and village settlements. In the case of concentrations, not only were persuasions and inducement involved, but compulsion as well.

When Swynnerton first argued the case for concentration as a way of dealing with the sleeping sickness problem, he proposed four incentives to induce people to move: 1) exemption from government-demanded work, 2) exemption from poll tax, 3) cleared land, and 4) plowed plots.

When he later suggested, however, that it was regrettable that more force could not be used, controversy arose.

The government asked for the opinions of provincial commissioners (PCs) on Swynnerton's suggestion. Those from both Central and Tabora Provinces expressed opposition to the use of compulsion.

In Central Province, the PC said that one must proceed with "the utmost circumspection" because the "whole economic and social equilibrium of the tribe might be upset by compulsory moves." Instead, he suggested that "by building huts and presents of small stock we should do everything to attract voluntary settlement ... but compulsory migration is a double-edged sword and may fearfully maim or even destroy the native authority employing such a weapon" (PC, Central Province, 1928).

In Tabora Province, the PC argued that force should not be used because the natural attraction of the settlements with schools, dispensaries, and freedom from tsetse flies was sufficient to entice people (PC, Tabora, 1928).

As a result, a policy was established in 1928 that limited the forced movement of people to significant cases involving sleeping sickness or "prejudicial congestion" of men or cattle (Chief Secretary, 1928). The controversy eventually led to the celebrated Circular No. 40 of 1934, in which Chief

Secretary Mitchell sought to define more explicitly

the government position on the issue:

> *I have heard a certain amount*
> *lately about our "concentration*
> *policy," which aims at inducing*
> *natives to settle in productive*
> *areas and develop them, rather*
> *than to eke out a precarious*
> *livelihood in unproductive areas.*
> *Stated in those terms the policy is*
> *unexceptionable and deserving of*
> *full support; but there seems, and*
> *not unnaturally perhaps, to be a*
> *certain measure of variety in the*
> *interpretation accorded to such*
> *words as "inducement and*
> *persuasion" legitimately pass into*
> *compulsion in certain*
> *circumstance, or can it not*
> *(Circular No. 40)?*

The answer was that it could, but only in such

exceptional circumstances as the presence of famine,

serious crimes such as cattle raiding, persistent danger to life, or endemic diseases and tsetse flies (Circular No. 40).

All three techniques were employed. An example is a case from Western Province during 1936-37. At a public meeting attended by the acting chief of secretary, the provincial commissioner, and the district commissioner, the people were told that they would have to move to a concentration being established nearby.

The people who had gathered responded with several of their own demands: that they are permitted to remain together under their chief, that the government promise not to forcibly move them again, that food assistance be given, and that a hospital be built.

Government leaders accepted all the requests except that for a hospital. In addition, they agreed to exempt the people from the hut and poll tax for a year, to transport their possessions at government expense, and to build a house for their chief.

Although most of the people moved, some fled toward the west and had to be brought back forcibly (Surveyor Macquarie, 1937). Persuasion, inducement, and compulsion were combined in this effort.

In the case of village settlements, recruitment campaigns were launched in various parts of the country to persuade people to join. When the response appeared to be insufficient, two additional steps were taken. First, promises of free food and "other delights" were made as incentives to induce people to apply for the settlements (Ellman, 1969, p. 3).

Second, the criteria for selection were not rigidly applied. Instead, members often were recruited by regional officials to solve their own problems of unemployment in towns and overpopulation in other areas (Newiger, 1968, p. 261).

As a result, many of those who joined were not really interested in making the settlements a success. In Ellman's words, the settlers considered themselves "rather as temporary and underpaid employees on Government estates, whose aim was to do the least possible work to exploit the Settlement Agency for what they could get out of it" (Ellman, 1969, p. 3; Nellis, 1972, pp. 125-126).

McHenry (1979) was of the opinion that for selective recruitment (e.g. in the case of the village settlement scheme), persuasion and inducement are sufficient and that for general recruitment (e.g. In the case of the concentration policy), compulsion is necessary.

POLITICIZATION OF

SETTLERS

Once the villages had been established, little effort was made in the concentrations to directly politicize the settlers to accept values necessary for the development of the village. Nellis criticizes leaders for not recognizing that politicization is a long-term proposition (Nellis, 1972, p. 128).

Organization of Production

Although in some concentrations an attempt was made to regulate rotation of crops, such efforts were said to have "not only failed but produced discontent and unrest, with a tendency for settlers to run away into the bush, where it was difficult to find them" (Fairbairn, 1944, p. 24).

In the village settlements, there was more control over the unit of production. There was a tendency toward individual plots in block farms which would involve more and more cooperatively undertaken tasks (Ellman, 1969, p.2).

The recruitment propaganda in 1963 suggested a target income per family of 150 Sterling Pounds ($429). In 1963-64, the Village Settlement Agency paid 100 Sterling Pounds ($286) and in 1964-65, it paid 68 Sterling Pounds ($194), but in neither year was the actual income from the sale of the crops near these levels. Rather, the Village Settlement Agency estimated what it thought was necessary to keep the settlers involved.

Payment was neither directly tied to the amount or quality of work nor to the communal production success (Thomas, 1966).

Getting People to Work

Together:

Pre-*Ujamaa*

Village Policies

A major problem with the implementation of the village settlement policy was the post-settlement task of getting people to work together.

There was considerable disagreement as to the extent of joint work prior to the intrusion of colonialism. In Nyerere's paper outlining the *ujamaa* village policy in 1967, he stated that working together was a basic aspect of traditional African family life. Others have argued that the scope and form of such labor was not the same as that demanded by the

ujamaa policy. One Tanzanian scholar has observed:

> *Ujamaa— in the strict sense of 1)
> communal production, 2)
> equitable sharing of communally
> produced goods, and 3) communal
> ownership of the means of
> production ... was possible only at
> the primary family and, in some
> cases, extended family levels.
> What existed beyond these levels
> was ujima rather than ujamaa.
> Ujima is a Swahili word which
> refers to the habitual practice of
> the cooperation of villagers in
> creation "peak" seasons ... or in
> cases of emergency (Mushi, 1971).*

WORKING TOGETHER:

COOPERATIVES

When modern ideas of cooperative work spread to Africa in the 1920s and 1930s, Tanzania was one of the first countries on the continent to encourage the movement.

In the 1920s, the Kilimanjaro Native Coffee Planters Association was established among coffee growers in the Moshi area (Digby, 1951, p. 148). This cooperative (later to be known as the

Kilimanjaro Native Cooperative Union) became one of the most powerful cooperative organizations in Africa.

The government sought to regulate the growth of cooperatives through the Cooperative Societies Ordinance, passed in 1932.

Its attitude toward cooperative expansion, however, was ambiguous. Government assistance to the cooperative movement took the form of advice, training, and encouragement.

Persuasion was an effective mechanism to get many peasants to work together in cooperatives, but it was not sufficient to induce them to apply their labor to tasks set by the government.

WORKING TOGETHER:

LABOR

The application of joint labor to achieve policy objectives during the colonial period was the subject of considerable controversy.

The question and answer appeared to be least costly and most beneficial ways to get people to work together for one particular end.

The technique used for gaining compliance was partly reflected in the terms used which include communal labor, tribal turnout, requisitioned labor, conscripted labor, and forced labor.

Forced labor had been ended after World War I by Article 5 of the League of Nations mandate, which state that the mandatory (Great Britain) would "prohibit all forms of forced or compulsory labor, except for essential public works and services, and then only in return for adequate remuneration" (Chidzero, 1961, p. 257).

The prohibition was reaffirmed in the International Labor Organization (ILO) convention, which was made applicable to the territory in the early 1930s.

The convention was interpreted to mean that the government could not use force to gain the labor it required to implement policies except for what might be considered "minor communal services." The colonial administration, however, devised various methods of circumventing such restrictions and applying the full range of compliance techniques.

Factors Affecting Settlement Implementation during Colonial and Early Independence Periods Many factors affected policy implementation in settlements during the colonial and independence periods. These factors were social, economic, political, and administrative. The following are the main factors:

1. The population of Tanzania consists predominantly of peasant cultivators. The 1967 census found 86 percent of the country's households engaged in farming (Koley, 1973, p. 151).

2. Economic differentiation in rural areas has developed to only a moderate extent. Issa Shivji has argued that though the wealthier peasants may have been politically important in a few local areas, they never played a significant role nationally (Shivji, 1975, p. 51).

3. Substantial ethnic diversity characterizes the Tanzanian population. Both the party and the government have worked hard to reduce the impact of 'tribalism.' In the 1967 census, 130 ethnic groups were recognized (Egro and Henin, 1973, p. 160).

4. The migration of peasant cultivators has characterized Tanzania for many years. Two types of movement of the rural population have occurred in Tanzania – that within rural areas and that from rural to urban zones. A high percentage of the migrants to urban areas consisted of youths (Sunday News, August 10, 1975, p. 6).

5. The African population of Tanzania has been growing rapidly. Although arable land is still available, this increase has put a considerable burden on the government to provide more services and opportunities (Tanganyika, African Census Report, 1957).

6. A substantial amount of unused land remains available for development in

Tanzania. Tanzania is a country of great physical variety, ranging from a long coastline to an extensive plateau to high mountain ranges to vast lakes. Estimates of the extent of cultivated land range between 5 and 10 percent of the total land area (Tanzania, Statistical Abstract, 1970).

7. The agricultural sector of the economy has been virtually stagnant for the past decade. Part of this stagnation is a consequence of the low crop prices accompanied by marked inflation (Tanzania, Statistical Abstract, 1970).

8. Government control over the economy has increased significantly since independence. Increasing state dominance of the economy suggests the parallel growth of the central government power and an expected decline in the vigor of opposition to the ujamaa policy (Tanzania, National Accounts of Tanzania 1964-1972, Dar es Salaam: Bureau of Statistics, February 1974).

9. The Economy of Tanzania is dependent to a great extent on trade with capitalist countries. Thus, Tanzania is tied closely to the world capitalist economy. Along with the flow of goods come Western managers, technicians, and ideas, and it is virtually impossible to implement policies that aim to establish self-reliant states (Leys, 1975; Shivji, 1976; Brett, 1973).

Agents of Implementation: The Party

Until early 1977, the sole political party on mainland Tanzania was the Tanganyika African National Union (TANU). In 1965, major constitutional changes had been made in TANU. The organization of TANU was based on territorial units (see the Appendix). However, functional or "place-of-work" TANU branches also existed. Policemen joined TANU as a police branch, TANU branches were started in the military, and there are TANU branches with pilot agricultural projects.

TANU had both elected and appointed officials, and different TANU organs (bodies) made up primarily of elected or appointed members.

The National Conference had its elected President and Vice President (of the party), and the National Executive Committee (NEC) was an elected body.

The Central Committee of the Party and the National Headquarters members were appointed or ex officio; regional, district, branch, and cell organizations had both elected and appointed members (Bienen, 1970, pp. 81-84).

However, TANU's combination with the Afro-Shirazi party from the island of Zanzibar under the new name Chama cha Mapinduzi (Party of the

Revolution) (CCM) has not fundamentally altered the characteristics of the party that evolved over nearly a quarter century.

It should be noted that the key to the success of any party involved with any policy implementation in a poor country is its relationship or linkage with the people. There are various aspects of the party through which the linkage may be examined.

In Tanzania, party membership was crucial. For example, membership was almost a prerequisite if one wants to obtain a license, to have a court case heard or need services.

Between 10 and 25 percent of the country's population are TANU party members (Finucane, 1974, p. 63).

Moreover, there are many structural layers between the members of the party and the central decision-makers. The Executive Committee of the party is the highest functioning committee of the party. One of the decisions of the party was the Arusha Declaration of February 1967 which gave birth to the guidelines of Tanzanian Socialism (Msekwa, 1973, p. 61).

Because of the many structural layers between the members of the party and the central decision-makers, the average party member has difficulty in making his voice heard in the important decision-making bodies of the party. A high proportion of the members of most party structures (from cell to

national level) are not directly elected (TANU, The
Constitution of TANU, 1973).

The top leadership of the party is able to
impose criteria for recruitment to political office.
Candidates for the National Assembly (the body that
legislated laws) and other TANU offices must be
approved by party structures at higher levels. The
National Assembly was formerly a standing
committee of the National Annual Conference of the
party which comprises the President of the party, the
Vice President and members of the National
Executive Committee of the party (Daily News,
October 4, 1975, p. 1).

Yet there are subtle forms of resistance against
the policies of TANU in the country. There has been

open opposition at times in the National Assembly.
Critics have been silenced, either by quick repression
or opposition in the National Assembly or by
detention orders (Daily News, April 26, 1975, p. 1).
The struggles for domination of the state by the party
and government have led to de jure supremacy of the
party in the policy formation but de facto domination
of government in policy implementation. The links
between the party and the government are normally
forged by the party in an effort to attain its objective
of overseeing the implementation of its policies
(TANU, Taarifa, November 1967, April 1969, and
1971; and Daily News (Dar es Salaam), June 9, 1975,
p. 1, respectively).

Agents of Implementation: The Government

Since independence in 1961, the country has gone to the polls four times to elect members of parliament from which government cabinet ministers are appointed by the President. Elections were held in 1965, 1970, 1975 and 1980.

The government that was formed after the 1965 election saw the birth of Tanzanian Socialism guidelines when they were first announced at Arusha (northeast of Tanzania) on February 5, 1967. The leader of the government has always been the leader of the party, and cabinet ministers are either party member elected to the National Assembly or appointed by the President (who is also the President of the Party). Whereas, as noted before, the party is involved in policy formation, the government is faced with the task of implementing it.

Through the years since independence, there has been a continuous modification of the structure of administration in the country. This has interfered with the establishment of stable patterns of popular participation. Changes of administrative structures have been frequent.

For example, the ward became an administrative area in 1969 with its own ward executive officer and ward development committee

(By Ward Development Committee Act No. 6 of 1969).

Because of the way the administration is formed, popular participation in decision-making has remained very limited.

Decisions are either made by the central machineries of the party or top hierarchy of the government which in turn work directly or indirectly together (Kundi, 1976, p. 39; Mayaya, 1976, p. 54; Lobulu, 1976, p. 46; Mosha, 1976, p. 64).

Politico-administrative officers tended to adopt the style and function of government officers. Shortly after independence, the offices of regional and area commissioners were established as the principal representatives of the central government and as the party secretaries of their respective areas. Their functions were basically the same as had been those of the provincial and district commissioners except for the removal of magisterial and some local government powers (Dryden, 1968, p. 23; and Finucane, 1974, p. 108).

When the regional and arena commissioner structures were established, administrative positions – those of administrative and area secretary, respectively – were created to assist them.

With decentralization in 1972, these officers were replaced by development directors at both levels but they were subject to the final overall policy direction and control from Dar es Salaam. As a result, administrative officers have generally dominated government structures at the regional and district levels.

In each district and region are representatives of the functional ministries. Because of staffing problems, not every area had its full complement of officers, and reorganizations of ministries resulted in further instability.

By the early 1970s, officers for health, education, natural resources, water, land development, public works, industries, agriculture, and cooperatives had been installed at most regional and district levels.

These officers have had considerable difficulty in promoting rural development (Nyerere, 1972, p. 4).

Yet observers are blaming "bureaucratization" for the difficulties government and party face when seeking to implement policies requiring the active compliance of the people. The most salient characteristic of Tanzania as it has evolved in the first decade and a half since independence is the growing predominance of government.

Rural bodies have been reduced in power, absorbed, or suppressed. Shivji argues that as in the case of the Soviet Union, a "bureaucratic bourgeoisie" is emerging (Shivji, 1975, p. 88).

THE GOALS OF *Ujamaa*

VILLAGES

The goals of *ujamaa* villages are also specified

in village constitutions. These are:

1) *To enable villagers to uplift their standard of living by:*
   a) *Including the spirit of hating all kinds of exploitation and instead building and maintaining the spirit of working cooperatively for the good of all members.*
   b) *Giving every villager an opportunity to work which gives him a just return, because work is the right and responsibility of every human being.*
   c) *Expanding the economy of the village by starting ujamaa farms, ujamaa shops, ujamaa activities, provided they are for the benefit of the village.*

d) *Selling the crops or any other goods produced in the village.*

e) *Buying and/or building and maintaining building, offices, industries, machines, and other equipment necessary for village development.*

f) *Cooperating with other activities so that no conflicts arise with the village leadership and the TANU creed and objectives.*

g) *Giving the villagers an opportunity to obtain education, medical care, and other necessities for the life and well being of man.*

h) *Setting an example to other citizens who have not joined so that they may like the* ujamaa *way of living together and working for the common good.*

i) *Accomplishing these aims or any one of them provided they do not contradict the TANU creed and objectives.*

1) *To give security of life to the villagers by:*

a) *Strengthening and consolidating the socialist spirit of brotherly love and respect.*

b) *Planning and incorporating all members into socialist work and distributing income according to the work done.*

c) *Saving money in the bank or elsewhere for future use.*

d) *Taking care of the aged, widows, orphans, and those who meet misfortune.*

e) *Lending money or sponsoring credit to villagers (Katiba Ya Kijiji cha Ujamaa – Ujamaa Village Constitution – mimeo; District Cooperative Office: Mufindi and Iringa).*

The Villages and Ujamaa Villages Act of 1975 (in Tanzania) specified three objectives for ujamaa villages:

1. To build a society in which all members have equal rights and opportunities and in which all members have gradually increasing basic level of material welfare before an individual lives in luxury.

2. To develop new socialist organization of labor and application of the principle of tying income to efficiency to eliminate every form of exploitation in collective production and to allow residents of ujamaa villages to develop their activity and creative initiative to the full.

3. To promote a spirit of self-reliance in social and economic activities such as by building schools, dispensaries, and the like (Government Notice No. 168, 1975, sec. 8).

In 1975, the Villages and <u>Ujamaa</u> Villages Act was passed. The Act required that Every Village be registered. To be registered, the village had to have established boundaries and, with a few exceptions a minimum of 250 households. The Act also mandated a uniform village government structure.

CHAPTER FOUR: COMMUNICATION AND THE TANZANIAN EXPERIMENT

The use of persuasion to motivate the rural population did not begin in 1967 with the ujamaa (family hood) policy. It had been used extensively by extension staff during the colonial period. The key mechanism for bringing about agricultural change in the 1950s was persuasion (Ruthenberg, 1964, p. 60). During the early 1960s (post-independence period), it was the most important tool at the disposal of party and government officials in rural areas.

The technique of persuasion used in Tanzania could be divided into four components. There were

[149]

those who persuade (the sources of the persuasive message). Then there is information which is transmitted. Third, there are the means by which the message is sent (the medium of communication), and lastly, there are the people who are to be persuaded (the object of persuasion).

THE SOURCE

President Nyerere was the most important
source of messages calling for people to move into
villages. He persuaded peasants to join the villages
and leaders to help implement the policy. Presidential
Circular No. 1 of 1969, which dealt with the
implementation of the ujamaa policy, stated:

> *The first necessity is the education
> and training of TANU and
> Government leaders in ideology,
> purpose, and methods of
> establishing ujamaa villages. The
> basic text on which this training
> will be based is the policy statement
> Ujamaa vijijini (Socialism in
> villages), supplemented by the other
> writings included in Essays on
> Socialism and the introductions of
> Freedom and Unity and Freedom*

*and Socialism (Presidential
Circular No. 1 of 1969).*

President Nyerere was successful in enlisting a great variety of agents to pass the message to the peasants. The agents included the prime minister, the first vice-president , ministers, regional commissioners, area commissioners, the Umoja wa Wanawake wa Tanzania (UWT – Union of Women of Tanzania) chairman, TANU officials, and many others. They toured the regions exhorting people to move into ujamaa villages.

There was no organization in the whole country which was not enlisted as an agent to relay the message of Presidential Circular No. 1 of 1969. The organizations included schools, the cooperative movement, the National union of Tanzania Workers (NUTA), the National Service, the TANU Youth League, the National Development Corporation (a parent parastatal organization for all nationalized industries), the Christian Council of Tanzania, the National Muslim Council, the Catholic church, the chief justice, magistrates, and Lions Club members (McHenry, 1979, pp. 119-120).

THE MESSAGE

The messages in the Tanzanian experiment conveyed two ideas. First, they implied there was a high probability that benefits would accompany the mere act of living together. Second, they suggested that there was a slight possibility that government assistance would be received or government penalties would be avoided should people move into villages. The following are some examples of the persuasive messages used in the Tanzanian experiment:

THE ROLE OF NYERERE'S POLITICAL ASSOCIATES IN PROMULGATING UJAMAA

Nyerere was supported by his circle of associates and cabinet members who would repeat the messages about how good his brand of African socialism was. One of his stern supporters was Rashidi Kawawa who hailed from the southern part of Tanzania. He was at one time the prime minister and later the second vice president after Tanganyika and Zanzibar were unified. Mr. Kawawa was once quoted as saying:

"Living together is the first step in bringing development and battling the enemies of poverty, ignorance and disease" (Press release A/370/74,

[155]

January 30, 1974). The message was aimed at changing existing behavior.

Chairman of UWT (Union of Women of Tanzania): *"The way to get rid of degradation was to cooperate together in the work of ujamaa villages"* (Press release A/3081/73, November 18, 1973). The message was aimed at changing existing behavior.

Regional commissioner (Mara – southern Tanzania): *"The only shortcut toward development was through people living together in villages and working hard"* (Daily News (Dar es Salaam), December 10, 1974, p. 1). The messages aimed at changing behavior.

Prime Minister: *"The reason so many had not progressed was because they worked on their own and*

not in <u>ujamaa</u> villages" (Press release A/2971/73,
November 8, 1973). The message was aimed at
changing existing attitudes.

Regional chairman of TANU (Mbeya –
southern Tanzania): *"Those who oppose <u>ujamaa</u> will
regret it when they see those who accepted gaining a
high standard of living"* (Daily News (Dar es
Salaam), September 21, 1973). There was a threat in
this message. Still the aim was for people to change
their behavior

President: *"People who refused to join <u>ujamaa</u>
villages were retarding their own progress together
with that of the country as a whole"* (<u>Nationalist</u> (Dar
es Salaam), March 25, 1971, p. 1). This meant that

the people's attitudes were retarding their own
progress.

Prime Minister: *"The people of Kilimanjaro should not fear their farms being put together for that was not the only form of ujamaa"* (Press release A/2701/73, October 13, 1973).

The message aimed at painting a good picture of the government in the eyes of the people of Kilimanjaro who were reluctant in moving to other villages started by the Arusha Declaration.

Area commissioner (Mpanda – southwest part of Tanzania): *"TANU and the government had decided the only way to obtain rapid development was to live in ujamaa villages because in that way different necessities such as water, schools,*

[158]

dispensaries, could be provided" (Press release
A/1510/73, June 23, 1973).

The Party and government were seen as
benefactors of the people in caring about people's
necessities.

Minister for health: *"If people live together, it
would be easy for the government to provide the
necessities of health and education"* (Press release
A/2212/72, August 27, 1972). The message painted a
good picture of the Party and government as the
benefactor of the people.

First vice-president: *"Living together makes
possible rapid development and assistance"* (Press
release A/2929/72, November 1, 1972). The message

also paints a bright future picture of development, so that people can change their existing behaviors.

THE MEDIA'S ROLE

RE-EXAMINED

The spoken word remained the most frequently used medium of persuasion. Meetings were a common feature in the daily life of the Tanzanian, and formed a major way of effecting person to person communication.

Discussion groups were divided into three categories. Category one included the formal discussion groups as practiced within the country's formal learning system, i.e. schools, colleges, institutions, and the University. Category two included the non-formal but action oriented discussion groups. Category three included casual or leisure time discussion groups (Ng'wanakilala, 1981, pp.79-81).

The spoken word was also the subject of considerable criticism one of the main reasons was that people spent too much time discussing ideology. The President warned against "false promises" and "exaggeration." An editorial in the government-owned newspaper, the <u>Daily News</u>, in 1975 went so far as to argue that the spoken word could never serve as the medium for rapid rural transformation:

> *"Correct ideas come from social practice.... It follows that there can be no such thing as a revolution by exhortation. There can even be no such thing as a revolution by mere ideas or belief.... Leaders, who merely talk, very soon degenerate into*

liars, misleading the people in every way ..."

(Daily News (Dar es Salaam), October 16, 1975, p. 1).

According to Ng'wanakilala (1981, p. 45), the mass media in Tanzania as a development force, was been charged with the specific and crucial role of mobilizing the masses and consequently narrowing the communication gap between the mass media and the larger population, the Party and government. There is significant co-operation and understanding between the mass media and Party/government officers in development planning and implementation of development objectives.

The propaganda content of the Tanzanian press is evident not only in issues about the country's

[163]

development, but about events and situations outside that country. An analysis of editorials appearing in January 1977 was made. The content analysis provided the following information: First, 75% of the editorials dealt with the question of political liberation in Zimbabwe, Namibia and South Africa. Second, the editorials attempted to induce national mass participation through various means. Third, they attempted to initiate discussions or issue guidelines on national political development issues. Last, they attempted to develop or maintain a kind of Tanzania togetherness. The press in Tanzania has also tried to intervene more directly in development issues (Ng'wanakilala, 1981, p. 27-28).

The Standard spent half of its editorial space for news on or about Tanzania. Forty-one percent of this news was about Dar es Salaam where the paper's offices were situated. Dar es Salaam is also the largest city in Tanzania. Eight Percent of the news came from the area surrounding Dar es Salaam. Very little news came from Zanzibar – one percent. News about the Americas was also very small. News about Africa was slightly more than news from Asia and Russia combined – 16.5 and 11.5 percent, respectively. Others account for the remaining 18.5 percent.

The Nationalist and ***Uhuru*** were then Party newspapers. The letter is a Swahili language newspaper. Swahili is a lingua franca of East and

Central Africa. It is not a surprise then that 87 percent of all news in **_Uhuru_** was about Tanzania because the bulk of Swahili speakers and readers are in Tanzania. Sixty-two percent of this news was about Dar es Salaam while 23 percent was about the periphery – the hinterland of Dar es Salaam. News about the rest of Africa constituted 8.5 percent while Zanzibar, Asia/Russia and others had 2 percent each of the shares.

News about Tanzania amounted to 45 percent of the editorial space in **_The Nationalist._** News about Dar es Salaam totaled 37 percent of this, while news about the hinterland totaled only 5.5 percent. News from other parts of Africa amounted to 18.5 percent,

Asia/Russia followed with 13 percent, Americas with 11 percent and others totaled 12.5 percent.

This means that the three papers covered a lot about Dar es Salaam – the main city. It should be noted that 1967 was the year of the Arusha Declaration and that ***ujamaa*** villages were not a reality then.

The predominance of news about Dar es Salaam was mainly due to the fact that the central government and the party together with their main offices were situated in Dar es Salaam.

Most of the news reporters were also working from Dar es Salaam, given the lack of sufficient news correspondents in other parts of the country.

The following is a sample of headlines written by the government owned newspaper, (***Daily News,*** Fortman 1980, pp. 147-148), reporting progress of the *ujamaa* experiment:

"***Kabuku Ujamaa*** Village Prospers," Daily News, 12 January 1974.

"***Ujamaa Smashes Poverty,***" Sunday news, 13 January 1974.

"***Success Depends on Ujamaa Living – PM,***" Daily News, 31 January 1974.

"***Tabora: Charting a Brighter Future***" Daily News, 6 February 1974.

"***Peasants Start Communal Farms***" Daily News, 20 March 1974.

"Rungwe Has 308 Villages," <u>Daily News</u>, 10 May 1974.

"Mwongozo Named Best Village," <u>Daily News</u>, 12 May 1974.

"Msongola Best <u>Ujamaa</u> Village in Dar Region,"

<u>Daily News</u>, 10 June 1974.

"Kibwara Village Emerges From Pangs of 'Gongo'."

<u>Daily News</u>, 10 October 1974.

"PM Warns Dodoma Singida Peasants," <u>Daily News</u>, 15 April 1977.

"Two Utete Peasants Fined," <u>Daily News</u>, 18 April 1977.

"Morogoro Peasant Jailed Four Months," Daily News, 25 April 1977.

"Sokoine Gives Direction on Famine Relief," Daily News, 1 May 1977.

"Experts to Live in Villages," Daily News, 15 May 1977.

"UPE Must Succeed: Unwilling Parents to Penalized," Daily News,

"PM Urges New Village Leadership System," Daily News, 8 June 1977.

"Do It Again, Experts Tell Peasants" Daily News, 15 June 1977.

"Peasants Messages Censored," <u>Daily News</u>, 12 December 15 June 1977.

"Village Managers Appointed," <u>Sunday News</u>, 25 December 1977.

"Namtumbo: A Three-in-one Village," <u>Daily News</u>, 12 May 1978.

"Steps to Ensure CCM Meetings," <u>Daily News</u>, 19 May 1978.

"Mkatanga Picked as Best Village," <u>Daily News</u> 22 May 1978.

"Village managers Recruitment Put Off," <u>Daily News</u>, 26 May 1978.

"A Life Dedicated to Duty," <u>Daily News</u>, 15 July 1978.

"Regional Roundup," <u>Daily News</u>, 29 September 1978.

"Tanga's Best Village," <u>Daily News</u>, 9 August 1978.

"Operation Save Cotton in Morogoro District," <u>Daily News</u>, 2 October 1978.

"Regional Roundup," <u>Daily News</u>, 20 October 1978.

"Meeting Decries Red-tape," <u>Daily News</u>, 30 October 1978.

"Regional Roundup," <u>Daily News</u>, 6 November 1978.

"Reaping the Fruits of <u>Ujamaa</u>," <u>Daily News</u>, 17 November 1978.

"Korogwe Villagers under Fire," Daily News, 29 November 1978.

"Village Carved out of a Forest," Daily News, 30 November 1978.

"Mtwara Plans to Raise Crop Production" Daily News, 16 December 1978.

"Peasants Told to Move" Daily News, 30 December 1978.

"Sokoine Urges Higher Productivity This Year" Daily News, 2 January 1979.

An observation about the nature of the words used in the government-owned "Daily News" of Tanzania then, showed a trend or a tendency.

Those newspaper stories, appearing in the newspapers and mass media outlets, saying that this politician or that politician had urged people (and for that matter used the term "peasants" in defining or describing the people who were the target of the campaigns, had indicated in that verbiage that they were leaning towards socialism or the country's political system, them.

Tanzania had then quoted as urging people to move from this village to that village by the reporters of the government-owned Tanzanian newspaper, "Daily News" was reporting as saying that the creators of the reported messages were urging.

When one urges, they are pushing "it". When one urges, they are telling people move here or move there. Note to the nature of persuasion and propaganda in the words chosen for the headlines. The headlines were in support of the move into *ujamaa* villages and changing existing behavior.

Some of these headlines suggest that the government should be credited with the benefit of *ujamaa.* Examples of these headlines are: *"Ujamaa Smashes Poverty," "Success Depends on Ujamaa Living – PM," "Reaping the Fruits of Ujamaa," "Village Carved Out of a Forest,"* and *"Kabuku Ujamaa Village Prospers."* The verbs used in these headlines are indicative of commentary that is common in the opinion pages of a newspaper. But the headlines were for news stories. The way most of the headlines were worded was suggestive of persuasion.

The wording of the headlines also suggested or implied that the government and party were doing the right thing to introduce *ujamaa* or to urge people to live in *ujamaa* villages.

Radio Tanzania contributed to the villagization experiment in various ways. First, it helped through its program *"Limbo Ya Mnyonge"* (A Poor Man's Stick", which was a political education program aimed at increasing the political consciousness of the people. The main content of the program was *ujamaa.* It would air recording from *ujamaa* villages, it would report on how the villages were progressing and it would emphasize that *ujamaa* was the only way for development – thus the reason for the title *"A Poor Man's Stick."* Second, Radio Tanzania contributed to the experiment through the program *"Sauti Ya Chama"* (The Voice of the Party), which was essentially a mass mobilization and political education program prepared by the Party (Ng'wanakilala, 1981, pp. 37-39).

Social practice was an alternative medium to the press, spoken word and radio in Tanzania. It was increasingly emphasized as words seemed to lose their impact. Leadership behavior became an important channel for conveying the message that people should live in ***ujamaa*** villages. In late 1969, the party newspaper, ***Uhuru,*** under the heading "New Election Qualification," reported that the TANU national executive secretary, Pius Msekwa,

...said that there was an <u>Ujamaa</u> village in every district and since the task of the party is the construction of socialism in the rural areas through <u>Ujamaa</u> village candidates who will have nothing to do with these villages will not be considered for election.

It is possible for everybody to join an <u>Ujamaa</u> village even for people who are salaried employees and are living in urban centers.... All they have to do is to identify them with one in the same manner as they are identified with a village from where they come (<u>Nationalist</u> (Dar es Salaam), December 9, 1969, p.1).

THE OBJECT

The targets of persuasive messages in the Tanzanian experiment were those who were to implement the policy and those who were to move into villages. At each of the biennial conferences of TANU, the President has urged delegates to hold seminars "in order to achieve great strides in arousing the people's political consciousness" (Nationalist (Dar es Salaam), December 29, 1969, p. 1).

Such seminars played an important part in persuading TANU, government, and village leaders, but did not affect the scattered peasantry. The following examples are characteristic of seminars held throughout the implementation period.

At a month-long seminar in Manyoni district (northeastern Tanzania), the area commissioner called on a group of teachers to assist the implementation of the *ujamaa* village policy and "plant the seeds of *ujamaa* in the hearts of their students" (Press release A/479/73, February 25, 1973).

At a seminar in Lindi region (southern Tanzania), speakers called on doctors, medical assistants and nurses to cooperate more in the work of initiating *ujamaa* villages (Press release A/2927/72, October 23, 1973).

At a meeting in Dar es Salaam, the commissioner of *ujamaa* villages and cooperative development urged TANU Youth League branch leaders to encourage all schools to identify themselves

[180]

with *ujamaa* villages so as to prepare the youths for a future life in them (Daily News (Dar es Salaam), March 26, 1973).

At a two-day seminar in Bukoba (west of Tanzania), TANU, government, and religious leaders were "called upon to stamp out enemies of the campaign to move to *ujamaa* villages." They were also urged to "show an example to the people by being the first to move to the new villages" (Daily News (Dar es Salaam), February 12, 1974, p. 4).

Persuasion did have some success. While it was the dominant technique, about 5 percent of the rural population moved into *ujamaa* villages.

Moreover, some peasants were skeptical about the messages and saw a discrepancy between the words and the deeds of those urging movement into villages.

DISCUSSION AND CONCLUSION

President Nyerere had stated many times that *ujamaa* villages must be established by persuasion, and had frequently argued against the use of both force and inducement. However, in "Socialism and Rural Development," the President remarked that socialist communities "cannot be established by compulsion" (Nyerere, <u>Freedom and Socialism</u>, p. 356). In Circular No.1, he said that the establishment of *ujamaa* villages "cannot be done by force" (Cliffe et al. 1975). In "Freedom and Development" he asserted, "An *ujamaa* village is voluntary association of people who decide of their own free will to live

[183]

together and work together" (Nyerere, <u>Freedom and Socialism</u>, 1968b, p. 67).

In 1972, a writer in the Daily News (the government-owned newspaper) declared that "the use of force is absurd and, in Tanzania, out of the question. Coercion dehumanizes man and has the effect of alienating the people from the revolution" (Daily News (Dar es Salaam), August 22, 1972, p. 4).

However, the following year, on November 6, President Nyerere advocated force for getting people to move together. He made a crucial declaration: it was now an order for everyone to live in villages, and all had to move by the end of 1976 (Press release A/2944/73, November 6, 1973).

The Swahili-language party newspaper, *Uhuru*, reported that President Nyerere had called for them to move in *ujamaa* villages. The Daily News reported that the President had called for all rural inhabitants to move into villages. Two days after the announcement, *Uhuru* published an editorial which further confused the distinction the President was making:

> *Six years have now passes since the party officials announced the policy of living together in Ujamaa villages…. In all this time, the party has used the method of persuasion to get the people to move into Ujamaa villages so as to hasten development. Yet very many people still prefer the traditional way of life in which they live individually…. Mwalimu Nyerere at Mbulu*

recently...declared...that in three years time every rural citizen should be living in an <u>Ujamaa</u> village.... Those who were reluctant have been given enough time and their fear can no longer be tolerated.... The issue of living in <u>Ujamaa</u> villages is now an ORDER of the party (<u>Uhuru</u>, Dar es Salaam, November 8, 1973).

The same day, Daily News in an editorial did

likewise. It declared:

"Those who have been told about the policy but have not understood it, those who have been educated about it but are still reluctant and those who have heard about it but are still consciously or unconsciously opposed to it must be made to live with their fellow peasants in communal villages where they will have an even better chance of grasping the advantages of socialist living.

[186]

> *It would be an unsocialist and retrogressive gesture if all such elements swerve to be left behind in backwardness or if they were delayed getting even the most elementary social amenities simply because at present they do not understand what socialism is all about."*
> *Mwalimu's call is to say the least a call to arms (Daily News, Dar es Salaam, November 8, 1973).*

All in all, a large percentage of the rural population moved into *ujamaa* villages. In 1977 (ten years after the initiation of *ujamaa* village policy), over 90 percent of the peasantry had resettled in villages.

Persuasion alone did not lead to the mass influx of people into villages that the party and government desired. Raikes (1973, pp. 9-10) says that the party was not strong enough to carry out the **_ujamaa_** village policy using the technique of persuasion and that the government approach was not attuned to be successful. By 1972, persuasion and inducement no longer were drawing many people into villages. Then, the addition of military force changed the balance.

As villages developed, village leadership assumed an ever-larger share of responsibility for encouraging people to participate in communal work. The role of both external and internal leadership in persuasion was sometimes complicated by poor rapport between leaders and peasants.

In one instance this led to the killing of a regional commissioner. Dr. Wilbert Kleruu, the regional commissioner of Iringa (southern Tanzania) in 1971, was actively engaged in implementing the *ujamaa* village policy two years before the President made settlement in village a requirement of all peasants. He was killed on Christmas Day that year at *Makungugu ujamaa* village by Saidi Abdullah Mwamwindi, a wealthy peasant cultivator.

To the government and the party, the incident became a symbol. Klerruu was seen as "the country's first martyr in building and defending *ujamaa*" (Daily News, Dar es Salaam, September 21, 1973, p. 3). The reality indicates an approach to persuasion that critics claimed was widespread and counterproductive.

Most peasants complied with the use of force. The use of force was accompanied by renewed efforts to persuade and to demonstrate the benefits of incentives. The party and government leaders were able to carry out the operations without significant opposition. The policy had potential benefits which many peasants perceived.

CHAPTER FIVE:

POLITICAL PERSUASION AND PROJECTS IN HEALTH AND NUTRITION

Mass media campaigns have been used to persuade populations to bring about changes in nutrition and health in Third World countries.

There have been many examples of such projects. But for the purpose of this study, four countries were chosen and were compared to Tanzania.

The countries were Trinidad and Tobago, Kenya, Haiti, and Tunisia. Kenya and Tunisia have been chosen because they, with Tanzania, are African countries.

Haiti and Tanzania belong to the same low-income bracket and are among the poorest nations in the world. Trinidad and Tobago, Kenya and Tanzania were all British colonies at one point.

TRINIDAD AND TOBAGO

The Trinidad and Tobago Breastfeeding Campaign was conceived and implemented in 1974. It had the objective of publicizing the relationship between breastfeeding and both good nutrition and living standards. The media involved were radio, television, posters, newspapers, periodicals, and films. The campaign was coordinated by the Housewives Association of Trinidad and Tobago. Planned in the early months of 1974, the campaign was launched in May 1974.

Employees of the advertising agency involved received a three-page brief designed to describe the nutritional and economic aspects of breastfeeding and to convince them that they had a product worth selling.

Once the advertising texts and artwork for the campaign were developed, clinic staff members and other health personnel were also briefed about the project and brought up to date on the benefits of breastfeeding.

Radio and television spot announcements reiterated messages carried by newspapers, posters, and handbills. The campaign was managed by media professionals who coordinated nine television programs and a series of daily five-minute radio broadcasts (called "Keeping Abreast with Man's History") with press coverage.

Discussions among school children and community groups were also part of the campaign, as were both centrally located and mobile library displays.

A key element in the breastfeeding project was the donation of time, expertise, and services by advertising agencies, governmental departments, media, commercial firms, and private citizens. These gifts were supplemented by rate reductions and other production advantages.

On the basis of its evaluation, the Caribbean Food and Nutrition Institute (CFNI) staff affirmed the effectiveness of the multi-media approach. The team further recommended that even more time and space in the mass media be devoted to this vital issue (Leslie, 1977).

The Ministry of Health was an agent of persuasion in the Trinidad and Tobago campaign. The decision to make breastfeeding the priority was made on the advice from Dr. Byam of the Ministry of Health. Dr. Byam was thus the source in the political persuasion.

In April 1974, the Minister of Health pledged his ministry's support for the campaign. It was launched on May 31, 1974 with the backing of the Ministry of Health and Caribbean Food and Nutrition Institute (CFNI).

Another agent in the persuasion was the Trinidad and Tobago Publishers and Broadcasters

Association which promised cooperation in the form

of time and space on radio, television and in the press

for a six-week period. Five 15-minute Government

Broadcasting Unit features were made after nurses

and mothers in clinics were interviewed and recorded

by Alfred Aguiton and Astra Da Costa, All Media

Projects Ltd. (AMPLE). The features were the

messages of persuasion. Alfred Aguiton and Astra Da

Costa, All Media Projects Ltd. (AMPLE) also

arranged a telephone conversation between HATT's

president, Mrs. Faith Wiltshire, and Mrs. Manley,

wife of then Prime Minister of Jamaica, who also

endorsed the program. The Ministry of Health

arranged a briefing session for health office personnel,

so that they would have up-to-date information on

breastfeeding. They also printed handbills and posters and were responsible for their distribution to health centers.

Ministry personnel assisted with television and radio programs. The Ministry of Health supplied paper and the Central Statistical Office of the government printed the handbills that were used in the campaign. The Central Statistical Office was thus an agent of persuasion, too.

Allison white, in a letter to the author, dated May 31, 1982, as Vice-President of the Housewives Association of Trinidad and Tobago (HATT), indicated that ever since 1974 there has been a heightened awareness of the superiority of breast milk.

The issue was kept alive by the press in Trinidad and Tobago, which took every opportunity to produce positive information on breastfeeding. The Trinidad and Tobago government was represented at a high level at the Geneva meeting on the World Health Organization code – as was a representative of HATT. Other groups were actively promoting breastfeeding – the Trinidad and Tobago Group of Nutritionists and Dietitians held three Nutrition Weeks in which breast feeding was highlighted, especially during the international year of the Child when T-shirts with "Best fed – Breast fed" were printed.

An organization with similar objectives to those of La Leche League was been formed. This was called the Trinidad and Tobago Informative

Breastfeeding Service (TTIES). Professional women in Trinidad and Tobago were taking breastfeeding more seriously then. Breastfeeding was being actively promoted throughout the Caribbean region.

Political persuasion played a role in making the breastfeeding campaign a success. The Ministry of Health (a department of the ruling government) was very cooperative. Five 15-minute Government Broadcasting promo features (with messages of persuasion) were made after nurses and mothers in clinics were interviewed and recorded, beside printing handbills and posters and being responsible for their distribution to health office personnel, so that they would have up-to-date information on breastfeeding.

Ministry of Health personnel assisted with television and radio programs. The Ministry also supplied paper and the Central Statistical Office printed the handbills which were used in the campaign.

In this way, the government in power was seen in good light by the people. The situation in Trinidad and Tobago was different from that in Tanzania due to the fact that there was less ideology in Trinidad and Tobago.

KENYA

A comedy troupe was used as an agent of persuasion in a radio campaign to change people's nutrition and health habits in delivering and raising children in Kenya in 1975. The voice of Kenya radio was the medium for the message in the campaign.

The message was contained in the show *"Zaa Na Uwatunze"* (Giving Birth and Caring for Your Children), which was created by an American, Mark Harris, working with UNICEF.

He had seen the comedy troupe and thought its delivery would be just right for the simple health information he felt needed to be broadcast to every region of Kenya where people often live in remote and decentralized villages and compounds (Kaufman, 1975).

UNICEF, the United Nations Fund for Population Activities, and the Voice of Kenya agreed to co-produce entertaining health education programs for open broadcast. As producers, the Voice of Kenya, UNICEF, and the United Nations Fund for Population Activities were the sources of the message of persuasion.

The series, which grew out of collaboration of the three organizations, featured nationally-known entertainers in an episodic situation comedy.

The presentations covered down-to-earth subjects – the nutritional value of eggs, the dangers of entrusting infants to the care of young siblings, and the need for inoculation – and gave listeners a chance to identify with both the situations and the characters.

The impact of the *"Zaa Na Uwatunze"* broadcasts has been calculated primarily in the terms of the size of the listening audience, listeners' recall of health information, and their familiarity with the characters.

Fan mail for the characters on the *"Zaa Na Uwatunze"* has been received from listeners in several East African countries besides Kenya. The *"Zaa Na Uwatunze"* series has been replicated in both Tanzania and Zambia with success (Hostetler, 1976). The Voice of Kenya (VOK), which broadcasted both radio and television, was under the direct control of the Ministry of Information. The

Ministry, which is a department of the government, had operated the Voice of Kenya since 1964. Given the illiteracy of the nation, and the ability of radio and television to reach millions, VOK was a powerful tool for education and propaganda and thus a powerful tool for persuasion.

Since the VOK was government-controlled, the *"Zaa Na Uwatunze"* was an example of political persuasion.

Therefore, any political alignment which the VOK may have had must have or should have been in line with the ruling government's political and ideological motives since VOK was owned by the Kenyan government. Although newspapers in Kenya may have been commercially owned – even by foreign investors – radio and television broadcasting was the exclusive province of the government (Wilcox, 1982).

The show was a success. This can be inferred from the fact that the show was replicated in both Tanzania and Zambia with success, and that fan mail for the characters was received from listeners in several East African countries besides Kenya.

The role played by the government in *"Zaa Na Uwatunze"* was covert. It should be noted here that although Kenya was a one-party state like Tanzania and other third world countries, it was not practicing the socialist ideology which her neighboring country Tanzania was bathed in implementing a communist oriented socialism called *ujamaa.*

[206]

The propaganda from the Tanzanian media was really cynical of the capitalist style in neighboring Kenya. The adjectives used by DJs and announcers on Radio Tanzania would compare capitalists to vampires or suckers of blood. Even when Julius Nyerere translated William Shakespeare's "Merchants of Venice" into the Swahili version which he entitled "Mabepari Wa Venisi" he gave the impression that the English word "Merchants" was the same as "Mabepari" which literally meant "Capitalists."

An impartial logical intellectual mind would question the literary butchering of a literal masterpiece like "Merchants Of Venice" into such a political downgrading by an African who had not written any literature, poem, play or novel like Nyerere himself.

To use your government owned radio station to brand your neighbor's governing style to the level of practicing vampire economic politics was as low as being a duck stuck in the sand also with its head in the sand while trying to catch flies in the air.

Kenya then was a system of government which was less ideologically oriented then her southern neighbor.

The role of the government in making the show a success could be seen in the fact that VOK agreed to co-produce the show, and air it, all the time it has been going on. This had an effect of building a positive image of the government in the eyes of the

audience.

HAITI

A campaign aimed at providing information and advice on family planning, nutrition, common illnesses, maternal and child health, and related topics, was started in Haiti in 1967. Its name was "Radio Doctor" and its target were Haitian adults of reproductive age, numbering roughly 2,500,000 men and women.

The campaign was conceived by Dr. Ary Bordes in 1967 when Hurricane Flora temporarily ended all broadcasting in Haiti, save the single station, Radio Lumiere. The disaster bred a new appreciation of the nationwide reach of the sole functional station, and Bordes vowed to make the most of the capability after the deluge.

Within a few months of the storm, "Radio Doctor" broadcasts commenced. Radio, cassettes, print, and visual aids were used in the campaign. These were the media for the messages of persuasion. All persuasive messages which had been developed on four topics – prenatal care, the new mother, infant health, and family planning were broadcast uninterrupted in the waiting rooms of clinics.

Twice a day, six days a week, Haitians used to tune in "Radio Doctor" on either Radio Lumiere or Radio Nationale in Creole, the local language. Radio seemed a natural choice for getting out health information and doctors' recommendations in Haiti.

Estimates on the number of transistors in the country varied from 85,000 to 300,000. A total of 99 of the nation's 1,500 rural schools have access to radios, and the sight of a Haitian with a transistor in hand was commonplace (Hollant, 1978, pp. 1-).

The Ministry of Health, which was one of the sponsors of the campaign, was also one of the sources of the persuasive message. The Ministry is a department of the government.

Thus the campaign had elements of political persuasion. It should be noted that by then the government was authoritarian, led by Dr. Duvalier, at a time when political opposition was not allowed in Haiti.

All traces of journalistic independence were stamped out during the most brutal years of Duvalier's dictatorship, 1957 to 1971 (Pierce, 1982).

The agents of persuasion in the Haitian campaign included the Ministry of Health, the Ministry of Education, Radio Nationale, and Radio Lumiere.

The Ministry of Health was one of the sponsors of the campaign, and so was the Ministry of Education. Radio Nationale, which was then owned by the government, was a non-profit operation and the Ministry of Health did not have to pay for broadcast time.

Radio Lumiere was a Protestant station. It was a network of six Christian radio stations in Haiti owned by the West Indies Mission (World Association for Christian Communication Newsletter, 1978).

Radio Lumiere and Radio Nationale were the two stations – media – for the messages of persuasion. That these stations could broadcast the "Radio Doctor" show each twice a day, six days a week, during the campaign and not charge for air time shows to some extent how supportive these stations were of the campaign.

A survey of a village of 4,000 that had heard the persuasive broadcasts for eight years indicated that knowledge of the subjects covered in the programs had risen dramatically.

Spot checks and other impressionistic evidence suggested that people committed the messages to memory. An in-school spin off of "Radio Doctor" entitled "Classe d'Hygiene" was successful. It was aimed at 30,000 fifth- and sixth-graders (most of them between the ages of ten and fifteen).

After 1975, "Radio Doctor" was institutionalized through the Education Department in order to reach both the teachers and the pupils of all Haiti's elementary schools. Working in the atmosphere created by the dictatorship of Dr. Duvalier, the persuasive campaign could not have preceded without government approval (or influence) since the government controlled most of the media.

The situation in Haiti was different from that of Tanzania. Radio Tanzania is owned by the government. In Haiti, Radio Nationale is owned by the government and Radio Lumiere is a network of six Christian radio stations.

In Tanzania, the latter was absent. Dr. Duvalier's dictatorial government did not lie down and ideology to be followed during the "Radio Doctor" campaign, while in Tanzania socialist ideology has to be followed according to the Arusha Declaration.

Media staff working in the Tanzania government and party-owned media must be members of the ruling party.

The government used the *"Radio Doctor"* campaign for educational purposes – to improve the health and nutrition of the Haitians. Indirectly, the government would have to be seen in good light by the people.

TUNISIA

A national survey conducted in 1975 by Tunisia's National Institute of Nutrition (NIN) showed that several nutritional problems plagued the poor majority of Tunisia. Resulting from this was the nutrition campaign whose main objective was to test the effectiveness of combining existing face-to-face education with inexpensive radio nutrition-education. Radio was selected as the medium for the campaign because it seemed the best means of reaching the largest number of rural mothers.

The radio messages were developed systematically and were pre-tested at local Mother and Child Health clinics (MCHs). Five basic themes were selected: the importance of exposing infants to sunlight, babies' need for supplemental feeding in the first year of life, the place of eggs and protein foods in the diets of healthy mothers and infants, the addition of vegetables to the infant's and mother's diet, and the importance of breastfeeding (CDC, 1979).

The impact of the educational campaign was investigated by means of interviews of mothers who attended the MCHs.

The project called for the selection of 16 clinics: eight clinics in which a half-day seminar would be given to midwives and nurses to reinforce the ongoing nutrition education and eight clinics in which radio broadcasts would not be supplemented with seminars.

A questionnaire was prepared and pre-tested for use at the end of six months of broadcasting to determine participants' knowledge, attitudes, and practices related to the five themes stressed in the project.

The value of the mass communication as part of an ongoing and nutrition-education program by the Tunisian and national institute of nutrition has been the most demonstrate of a success of the program. Data from a variety of sources, including both in and anecdotal comments and in-depth interviewing, indicate that the programs central character, Dr. Hakim, was a widely recognized figure in Tunisia. 88% of the mothers interviewed identified Dr. Hakim when asked who delivered the nutrition messages via radio.

Through Dr. Hakim, nutrition became a hot topic of general concern throughout the country. The ability of Dr. Hakim's program to reach Tunisian society has been concretely established. Along with responses to certain items on the evaluation questionnaire, clinic reports of sharp increases in the use of SAHA, a supplemental food are recommended in the radio programs, suggested that mothers' knowledge and perhaps even behavior were positively influence by the program. The self reported increases in early exposure of influence to some whites are positive signs of possible success (Agence de

Cooperation Culturelle et Technique, 1974, pp. 32-33).

Prior to the campaign, the National Institute for Nutrition and Food Technology and was formed within the Ministry of Public Health. This institute conducted a national survey in 1975 which showed that several serious interest in a problem to plague the poor majority of Tunisia. The Nutrition Institute person now believed that communication could make an important contribution to extending nutrition education to large numbers of rural poor. Operating under the direction of the Institute of Child Health of the Ministry of Public Health were the Maternal Child Health (MCH) centers.

The primary purpose of the centers was to provide a pediatric and gynecological for the low income population. Starting at huge center consisted of Physicians, midwives, nurses, and nursing aides.

The MCHs centers were thus agents in the political persuasion. And so was the umbrella Institute of Child Health of the Ministry of Public Health. Radio was the medium of persuasion. Nutrition education was the theme of the messages of persuasion. Dr. Hakim was the source of the messages.

The physicians, midwives, nurses and nursing aides at the MCH centers were also agents in the persuasive campaign. There was not ideology laid down by the central government to be followed by the campaign as in Tanzania during the villagization campaign.

In Tunisia, the primary purpose of the nutrition campaign was to provide pediatric and gynecological services for the low-income population. This function was carried under the umbrella of the Ministry of Health.

The Tunisian government's involvement was not as direct as that of the Tanzanian one. But it served its audience and thus reflected positively on the ruling government.

The medium that carried out the messages by Dr. Hakim was the Radiodiffusion Television Tunisienne (RTT) which was owned by the government.

The fact that RTT was government-owned was an advantage because RTT provided broadcast and other related services at no cost to the campaign.

Because of the nature of the Tunisian radio setup, there was no exact limit on the number of messages about nutrition which would be aired, nor did the RTT place any limit on the number of messages which would be aired (Munger, 1978).

CONCLUSIONS

In Trinidad and Tobago, there was a heightened awareness of the superiority of breast milk. The media kept the issue alive.

Many agencies, including the Housewives Association of Trinidad and Tobago (HATT), the Trinidad and Tobago Informative Breastfeeding service helped in making the campaign a success. Ministry of Health personnel assisted with television and radio programs.

In Kenya, the *"Zaa Na Uwatunze"* (Giving Birth and Caring for Your Children) show as successful, given that it was replicated in both Tanzania and Zambia with success. The show was educational like the breastfeeding project of Trinidad and Tobago. The information messages were aimed at changing the nutrition and health habits of the audience.

Radio played an important role to educate and persuade adults of reproductive age about family planning, health and nutrition in Haiti. People who listened to broadcasts committed the messages to memory, according to a survey of a village of 4,000 that had heard the broadcasts for eight years.

In Tunisia, there have been sharp increases in the use of supplemental food recommended in nutrition messages delivered via radio.

In the four countries, radio was the main medium of communication. The messages were educational, aimed at changing people's attitudes and behaviors about nutrition and health.

The roles played by the communication media were in line with the policies of the governments in power since radio in these countries is owned, partly owned, or controlled by the governments in power.

The effect of politics is present in these radio campaigns.

CHAPTER SIX:

A MODEL FOR POLITICAL PERSUASION IN A THIRD WORLD SETTING

There had been many problems in Third World countries. Most of these countries had been faced with the tasks of expanding schools, fighting disease and poverty.

These problems tended to be interrelated. A majority of Third World people lived in rural areas, making a marginal existence with work of low productivity.

Most governments wanted their masses of rural poor to *"modernize, become more productive, eat*

better, get basic education, produce fewer children, and have better health (McAnany, 1973).

Most rich countries then had 10 or 12 years of compulsory education and were then concerned about its quality. In the Third World, there were not enough schools to go around. Not even enough poor and inadequate schools (Young et al. 1980, pp. 3-5). Yet there was a need for human growth and development.

PARAMETERS

Many educational budgets were absorbing between 20 and 30 percent of governments budgets and it is difficult to see how they can expand further without cutting into other areas. There were the problems of disease and poverty, which limit development in these countries. Gross National Products are low. Government expenditures are high, thus creating national deficits.

Most of these countries were in Sub-Saharan Africa, and some of the more populated countries of Asia (namely India, Pakistan, Bangladesh, and Sri Lanka).

These countries had per capita incomes of less than $360 per year. While there were over 4 billion people in the world, 2.2 billion of these live in 39 countries whose per capita income is less than $360 per year (Hoogvelt, 1982).

The limits made by poverty tended to affect ignorance and disease. Poverty, ignorance and disease work in a vicious circle. As far as communication was concerned, there were a few papers and fewer TV stations.

Because of the limits of poverty, radio was advantageous for development communication. Political persuasion under the guise of development communication had been in use in Third World countries.

The main reason was to effect changes in the direction desired by the governments in power.

An example of political persuasion took place in Tanzania during the ***ujamaa*** (family hood) villagization program which started in 1967.

Towards a General Model for Political Persuasion in a Third World Setting

The Tanzanian _ujamaa_ (family hood)

villagization experiment was a rural development

project. Rural development was conceived as a

process of radical change in social relations leading to

new social formations in the rural society (Rahim,

1976).

Rural development in the People's Republic of

China and Tanzania made intensive use the

interpersonal channels by the political party cadres.

The message contents were predominantly ideological – the informational messages were always related and subordinated to ideological contents. For instance, the following story appears in a book specially compiled for the use of propagandists in the People's Republic of China. It was a model experience of a propagandist:

EATING NOODLES

"On a Saturday we had noodles…. At noontime all work a man came to the mess hall. While paying for his meow, one worker said in great delight: 'We have noodles to eat.'

"I (the propagandists) immediately added: 'that's right. Yesterday we had bread today we have noodles …. We're no longer in the days of the Japanese occupation, when we had <u>hsiang-tze-mien</u> date in and day out.'

"Because I mentioned this, all the people around me begin to remember the days in the past. Who had not suffered? Who wanted to live again the life of those days? Then why the (propagandist) said:

'now there are still people who will not let us keep this (noodles)!'

'Who?' people asked, before I had finished my sentence.

"*'Who? If the American doubles,'* I answered, and then continued: *'the American devils started the war of aggression in Korea because they wanted to invade China. Unless we lemonade the entire American devils, we shall have no good days in the future. In order to drive away the American devils, we have to speed up production and support the front....'* (Yu, 1963 p. 289)."

In Tanzania, at the party headquarters, there are two singing groups, each known by the name of the group leader. There is Magongoro the group and the Ng'wanakilala group. Their role in message

occasion and distribution of information or

multiplication of messages is significant.

One of Makongoro's songs is as follows:

The Second

Five Year Plan

> *Tells us that we*

> *should eat*

> *chicken, eggs,*

> *vegetables, and*

> *fish and also*

> > *drink milk it*

> *tells us that we*

> *should eat body*

> *building foods it*

[238]

tells us that we

should build

better houses.

The party has lit

the torch, Praise

to Nyerere!

Another singer and dancer, Juma Kahenke has composed the following song:

I have talked enough,

I have written enough

I am talking no more;

I should act to improve my living

Conditions...

(Ng'wanakilala, 1981, pp. 100-101)

Thus, the main function of development communication in such cases is promoting and heightening the political consciousness of the peasants and workers in the villages.

In Tanzania, the ideological messages in rural development communication originate from the Arusha Declaration of the ruling Tanganyika African National Union (TANU) party, and the essays on African socialism and socialist education written by Julius Nyerere. The theme of ideological messages is that the African socialist society is based on ujamaa or family hood. The village community is an extended family, with each individual worker contributing labor for the benefit of the community and with the community taking care of each member.

The rural population in Tanzania is constantly exposed to the ideological communication transmitted by the party cadres and government officials in interpersonal conversations, village meetings, and rural training centers. The people learn about the four kinds of evil exploitation – feudalism, capitalism, imperialism, and parasitism. They are persuaded to adopt the traditionally rooted, but newly conceptualized, socialist way of life based on the collective control of the major means of production, cooperative management, and self-reliance (Rahim, 1976).

The ruling party, TANU, assumed the primary responsibility for rural development communication. The basic unit of the TANU is the cell consisting of ten households. The main functions were (1) to bring peoples' problems and grievances to the party, and (2) to mobilize groups for the implementation of development projects.

The cell leader was the key communicator. He maintained close personal contacts with the individual members of the cell, mobilizes groups of members for development activities and provides feedback to the party and the government (Rahim, 1976).

Other studies, for example, on done in Chile, tend to confirm the importance of interpersonal communication. As reported by Brown (1970, pp.

725-734), the field experiment was carried out in Chile to test the effect of a specialized communication program which asked whether exposure patterns and effects are the same for a specialized "locally relevant" medium as for the "Western Model" mass media.

The study included a "treatment consisting of one-page mimeographed circulars mailed weekly from Santiago and a second survey to describe changes produced by 27 weeks of treatment. Among the findings were that illiterate subjects had access to the content of the circulars through literate friends or members of the households (usually the latter).

A secondary diffusion occurred via reading aloud, via lending of circulars, and via conversations.

Literates, and especially literate opinion leaders, were more active than illiterates in discussing the circulars outside their own households. Kinship and friendship – especially established visiting patterns – also played a role in secondary diffusion.

At this point, it is imperative to form a general model for political persuasion in a Third World setting. Poverty leads to ignorance due to lack of skills to increase production, to manage production, to market products, to plan for better growth and development. Ignorance affects disease. Education is vital in the prevention or cure of disease, in the proper nutrition of a society, or whole nation. Disease, on the other hand, can affect school age children and they would not be able to do well in school. An ailing nation cannot do very well in fighting ignorance. Disease affects the economy (it can increase poverty), for example an ailing nation does not produce what it should. Poverty blocks the effective fight against disease.

Lerner (1963, p. 346) defines the vicious circle of poverty as the situation in which no sustained economic growth is possible because each specific advance is rapidly checked by some counter-tendency in the social system. The most important of such counter-tendencies is excessive population growth.

The Tanzanian villagization program used political persuasion. Like many Third World countries, the Tanzanian experiment occurred in a setting of ignorance, disease and poverty. The following is a schematic summary of the Tanzanian experiment in terms of political persuasion.

The vicious circle is caused by the interlocking of poverty, ignorance and disease.

Levels of politicization differed from country to country. Although in the Third World the major concern of the governments in power was to use the media for rapid development of the masses, differences in ideology lead to different levels of politicization in the use of persuasion.

While in countries like Tanzania it was explicit that the government and party want the people to follow a socialist ideology in living together in ujamaa villages; in other countries such a thing is not very explicit.

In such countries, governments and their machineries carry out mass media campaigns to improve the living conditions of the people. As a result, the governments were seen as benefactors of the masses. Consequently, this would justify the government's stay in power. It could be asserted that such was the case in other countries such as Haiti, Trinidad and Tobago, Tunisia, and Kenya, although no government would openly admit it.

A modified model to reflect the different levels of politicization should look like the following:

CONCLUSION

Given that Third World countries are poor and also limited by ignorance and disease, many of them have chosen political persuasion to achieve desired goals. Tanzania is one of them with the villagization program. Tunisia, Kenya, Haiti, Trinidad and Tobago used political persuasion to achieve their goals of either better nutrition or health. Since most mass media in Third World countries are owned by the governments, political persuasion is made easier. The most widely used medium is radio because of its effectiveness, localness, time, and cost. The spoken word like speeches and seminars is also used widely.

BIBLIOGRAPHY

Agence de Cooperation Culturelle et Technique. La Vulgarisation Agricole en Tunisie, "Direct" (June 1974): 76.

American Association of Agricultural College Editors. Communications Handbook. Danville, Illinois: The Interstate Printers and Publishers, Inc., 1970.

Andersen, Kenneth E. Introduction to Communication Theory and Practice. Urbana: University of Illinois at Urbana, 1972.

Apted, F.I.C. Sleeping Sickness in Tanganyika, Past, Present and Future. Transactions of the Royal Society of Tropical Medicine and Hygiene 56 (1962): 16.

Bavu, Immanuel. Leadership and Communication in Ujamaa Process: A Case Study of Kabuku Ndani Ujamaa Village Cooperative Society. Unpublished Master's thesis, Department of Sociology, University of Dar es Salaam, 1971.

Barelson, B., Lazersfeld, P., and McPhee, W. Voting: A Study of Opinion Formation in a Presidential

Campaign. Chicago: University of Chicago Press, 1954.

Bienen, Henry. Tanzania: Party Transformation and Economic Development. Princeton, New Jersey: Princeton University Press, 1970.

Blau, P.M. and Scott, W.R. Formal Organizations. San Francisco, California: Chandler, 1962.

Brembeck, W.L. and Howell, W.S. Persuasion. Englewood Cliffs, New Jersey: Prentice-Hall, 1952.

Brett, E.A. Colonialism and Underdevelopment in East Africa. London: Heinemann, 1973.

Brown, Marion R. "Communication and Agricultural Development: A Field Experiment." Journalism Quarterly 47, No. 4 (Winter 1970): 725-734.

Chidzero, B.T.G. Tanganyika and International Trusteeship. London: Oxford University Press, 1961.

Chief Secretary to Acting Director of Game Preservation. TNA: 11771. May 17, 1928.

Circular No. 40 of the Tanganyika Government. TNA: 22494. 1934.

Condon, John. "National Building in the Tanzania Press." Journal of Modern African Studies, No. 53 (1967).

Daily News (Dar es Salaam), March 26, 1973.

Daily News (Dar es Salaam), September 21, 1973.

Daily News (Dar es Salaam), November 8, 1973.

Daily News (Dar es Salaam), February 12, 1974.

Daily News (Dar es Salaam), December 10, 1974.

Daily News (Dar es Salaam), April 26, 1975.

Daily News (Dar es Salaam), October 4, 1975.

Daily News (Dar es Salaam), October 16, 1975.

Digby, Margaret. Agricultural Cooperation in the Commonwealth. Oxford: Blackwell, 1951.

Dryden, Stanley. Local Administration in Tanzania. Nairobi: East African Publishing House, 1968.

252

Egero, Bertil and Henin, Roushidi. Distribution by Sex and Age in the Population of Tanzania. Dar es Salaam: Bureau of Resource and Land Use of Resource and Land Use Planning and Bureau of Statistics, 1973.

Eisenson, J. and Irwin, J. The Psychology of Communication. New York: Appleton-Century-Crofts, 1963.

Ellman, A.O. "Agricultural Improvements through Cooperative Farming in Tanzania: A Brief outline." University of Dar es Salaam, Economic Research Bureau Paper 69.23, p. 3, 1969.

Fairbairn, H. "The Agricultural Problem Posed by Sleeping Sickness Settlements." East African Agricultural Journal 9 (1943-44): 17.

Fairbairn, H. and Maclean, George. "The Relationship between Economic Development and Rhodesian Sleeping Sickness in Tanganyika Territory." East African Agricultural Journal 9 (1943-44): 41.

Findlay, Allan M., Findlay, Anne M. and Lawless, Richard I. Tunisia. Santa Barbara, California: Clio Press, 1982.

Finucane, James R. Rural Development and
    Bureaucracy in Tanzania: The Case of
    Mwanza Region. Uppsala: The Scandinavian
    Institute of African Studies, 1974.

Friedland, William H. and Rosberg, Carl G., Jr. (eds.).
    African Socialism. Stanford: Stanford
    University Press, 1964.

Georgulas, Nikos. "Settlement Patterns and Rural
    Development in Tanganyika." Occasional
    Paper No 29. Program of Eastern African
    Studies, Syracuse University, May 1967.

Government Notice No. 168, 1975.
Harbison, Frederick. "Education for Development."
    Scientific American 209, No. 3 (1963): 140.

Hollant, Edith. "On the Air." Salubritas 2, No. 2
    (1978): 1.

Hoogvelt, Ankie M.M. The Third World in Global
    Development. London: The Macmillan Press
    Ltd., 1982.

Hostetler, Susan. "Health Messages through Humor."
    ICIT Report, No. 15, July 1976.

Hyden, Goran. Beyond Ujamaa in Tanzania: Underdevelopment and Uncaptured Peasantry. London: Heinemann Educational Books, 1980.

Janowitz, Morris. "The Technique of Propaganda for Reaction: Gerald L.K. Smith's Radio Speeches." The Public Opinion Quarterly 8 (1944): 1.

Jensen, Soren and Mkama, Jumanne (compilers). District Data. Dar es Salaam: Ministry of Economic Affairs and Development Planning, 1968.

Kaplan, Irvin (ed.). Tanzania: A Country Study. Washington: American University, 1978.

Kaplan Irvin, Dobert, Margarita K., Marvin, Barbara J., McLaughlin, James L. and Whitaker, Donald P. Area Handbook for Kenya. Washington, D.C.: Foreign Area Studies, 1976.

Katiba Ya Kijiji Cha Ujamaa (Ujamaa Village Constitution). Mimeo. District Cooperative Office: Mufindi and Iringa, 1967.

Koley, Chinmoy. "Agricultural Data." In Bertil Egero and Roushidi Henin (eds.), The Population of Tanzania, Census Vol. 6. Dar es

Salaam: BRALUP and Bureau of Statistics, 1973.

Kundi, A.T. Popular Participation in Tanzania, A Case Study of Initiation and Implementation of Water Projects in Kirua Vunjo West Ward in Moshi District. Dissertation. Department of Political Science, University of Dar es Salaam, 1976.

Lazarsfeld, P.F., Berelson, B. and Gaudet, H. The People's Choice. New York: Duell, Sloan and Pearce, 1948.

Lazarsfeld, P.F. and Stanton F. Communications Research, 1948-1949. New York: Harper and Brothers, 1949.

Lerner, Daniel. "Towards a Communication Theory of Modernization: A Set of Considerations." In Communications and Political Development. Edited by Lucian W. Pye. Princeton, New Jersey: Princeton University Press, 1963.

Leslie, Joanne. Five Nutrition Projects That Use Mass Media. Development Communication Report, No. 20. Washington, D.C.: Clearinghouse for Development Communication, September 1977.

Leys, Colin. Under development in Kenya. London: Heinemann Educational Books, 1975.

Lobulu, W.N. Popular Participation, Control and Development: A Study of the Nature and Role of Popular Participation in Tanzania's Rural Development. Unpublished doctoral dissertation. Department of Political Science, Yale University, 1976.

Manoff, Richard K., Cooke, Thomas M., and Romweber, Susan M. Radio Nutrition Education – Using the Advertising Technique to Reach Rural Families: Philippines and Nicaragua. Washington, D.C.: Manoff International, 1977.

Mayaya, R.M Decentralization and Popular Participation in Shinyanga District. Dissertation. Department of Political Science, University of Dar es Salaam, 1976.

McAnany, Emile and Jamison, Dean. Radio for Education and Development. Beverly Hills, California: Sage Publications, 1978.

McAnany, Emile G. and Mayo, John K. Communication Media in Education for Low-income Countries: Implications for Planning.

Paris: UNESCO's International Institute for Education Planning, 1980.

McAnany, Emile G. Radio's Role in Development: Five Strategies of Use. Washington, D.C.: Information Center on Instructional Technology, Bulletin 4. Academy for Educational Development, 1973.

McGuire, W. "The Nature of Attitudes and Attitude Change." In G. Lindsay and E. Aronson (eds.) Handbook of Social Psychology. Reading, Massachusetts: Addison-Wesley, 1969.

McHenry, Dean E. Tanzania's Ujamaa Villages: The Implementation of a Rural Development Strategy. Berkley, California: Institute of International Studies, University of California, 1979.

Miller, G.R. and Burgoon, M. "Persuasion Research: Review and Commentary." In Communication Yearbook 2. Edited by B. Rubin. New Brunswick, New Jersey: Transaction, 1978, pp. 29-47.

Minick, W.C. The Art of Persuasion. Boston, Massachusetts: Houghton-Mifflin, 1957.

Moss, Manorama S. What Extension Educators and the Mass Media Can and Can't Do – A Nutrition Education Project in India. Development Communication Report No. 23. Washington, D.C.: Clearinghouse for Development Communication, July 1978.

Mott, Frank Luther. "Newspapers in Presidential Campaigns." Public Opinion Quarterly 18 (1944): 3

Msekwa, P. Toward Party Supremacy: The Changing Pattern of Relationships between the National Assembly and the National Executive Committee of TANU before and after 1965. Unpublished Master's thesis. Department of Political Science, University of Dar es Salaam, 1974.

Munger, Sara J. "Mass Media and Nonformal Nutrition Education – Final Study Report." Synectics Corporation, 4790 William Flynn Highway, Allison Park, Pennsylvania, 1978.

Mushi, Samwel S. Modernization by Traditionalization: Ujamaa Principles Revisited. Taamuli 1, No. 2 (March 1971): 22.

National Geographic Society. Atlas of the World. Washington, D.C.: National Geographic Society, 1981.

259

Nationalist (Dar es Salaam), December 9, 1969.

Nationalist (Dar es Salaam), December 29, 1969.

Nationalist (Dar es Salaam), March 25, 1971.

Nellis, John R. A Theory of Ideology: The Tanzanian Example. Nairobi: Oxford University Press, 1972.

Newiger, Nikolaus. Village Settlement Schemes: The Problem of Cooperative Farming in Smallholder Farming and Smallholder Development in Tanzania. Edited by Hans Ruthenberg. Munich: Weltforum Verlag, 1968.

Ng'wanakilala, Nkawbi. Mass Communication and Development of Socialism in Tanzania. Dar es Salaam: Tanzania Publishing House, 1981.

Nyerere, Julius K. Decentralization. Dar es Salaam: Government Printer, 1972.
Nyerere, Julius K. Freedom and Socialism. Dar es Salaam: Oxford University Press, 1968b.

Nyerere, Julius K. President's Inaugural Address in Nyerere, Freedom and Unity. Dar es Salaam: Oxford University Press, 1966.

Nyerere, Julius K. Socialism and Rural Development. Dar es Salaam: Government Printer, 1967.

Nyerere, Julius K. The Arusha Declaration. In Nyerere, Ujamaa: Essays on Socialism. New York: Oxford University Press, 1968a.

Nyerere, Julius K. Ujamaa: Essays on Socialism. Dar es Salaam: Oxford University Press, 1968c.

Ottaway, David. "Letter from Tanzania." Washington Post, May 24, 1975a.

Ottaway, David. "Tanzania: Peasants on the Move." Washington Post, May 18, 1975b.

Parlato, Margaret Burns. "Breaking the Communications Barrier." India: CARE, 1973.

PC of Central Province to Chief of Secretary. TNA: 11771. February 2, 1928.

PC of Tabora to Chief of Secretary. TNA: 11771. February 21, 1928.

Pierce, Robert N. "Haiti." In The World Press Encyclopedia. Edited by George Kurian. New York: Facts On File, Inc., 1982.

261

Pool, Ithiel de Sola. "The Mass Media and Politics in the Modernization Process." In Communications and Political Development. Edited by Lucian W. Pye. Princeton, New Jersey: Princeton University Press, 1963.

Pratt, Cranford. The Critical Phase in Tanzania, 1945-1968. Cambridge: Cambridge University Press, 1976.

Presidential Circular No. 1 of 1969. In Rural Cooperation in Tanzania. Edited by Lionel Cliffe et al. Dar es Salaam: Tanzania Publishing House, 1975.

Press Release A/1977/72, August 4, 1972.

Press Release A/2212/72, August 27, 1972.
Press Release A/2929/72, November 1, 1972.

Press Release A/479/73, February 25, 1973.

Press Release A/1510/73, June 23, 1973.

Press Release A/2701/73, October 13, 1973.

Press Release A/2927/73, October 23, 1973.

Press Release A/2944/73, November 6, 1973.

262

Press Release A/2971/73, November 8, 1973.

Press Release A/3081/73, November 18, 1973.

Press Release A/370/74, January 30, 1974.

Press Release A/1556/74, April 14, 1974.

Rahim, Syed A. "Communication Approaches in Rural Development." In Communication and Change: The Last Ten Years – and the Next. Edited by Wilbur Schramm and Daniel Lerner. Honolulu, Hawaii: The University Press of Hawaii, 1976.

Raikes, Phil. "Ujamaa Vijijini and Rural Socialist Development." Paper presented at East African Universities Social Science Conference, Dar es Salaam, 1973.

Reardon, Kathleen K. Persuasion: Theory and Context. Beverly Hills: Sage Publications, 1981.

Rogers, E., Brown, J., and Vermillion, M. "Radio Forums: A Strategy for Rural Development." In Working Paper 266, Radio for Education and Development: Case Studies, Vol. 2. Edited by Spain, P., Jamison, D., and McAnany, E. Washington, D.C.: World Bank, 1977.

Rogers, E. and Soloman, D. Radio Forums for Development. East Lansing, Michigan: Department of Communication, Michigan State University, June 1972.

Ruthenberg, Hans. Agricultural Development in Tanganyika. Berlin: Springer-Verlag, 1964.

Schramm, W. and Lerner, D. (eds.). Communication and Change in the Developing Countries: Ten Years After. Honolulu: University of Hawaii, East-West Center Press, 1976.

Sears, D. and Freedman, J. "Selective Exposure to Information: A Critical Review." Public Opinion Quarterly 31 (1967): 194-213.

Sears, D. and Whitney, R. "Political Persuasion." In Handbook of Communication. Edited by I. Pool. Chicago: Rand-McNally, 1973.

Shivji, Issa G. Class Struggle in Tanzania. Dar es Salaam: Tanzania Publishing House, 1975.

Sunday News (Dar es Salaam), August 10, 1975.

Swynnerton, C.F.M. to Chief Secretary. TNA: 2702, Vol. 2. March 17, 1924.

Tanganyika African Census Report, 1957. Dar es
Salaam: Government Printer, 1963.

Tanzania, Dar es Salaam. Quarterly Statistical
Bulletin 26, No.1 (June 1975): sec. 1.

Tanzania. National Accounts of Tanzania, 1964-
1972. Dar es Salaam: Bureau of Statistics,
February 1974.

Tanzania. Statistical Abstract. Dar es Salaam: Dar
es Salaam Printer, 1966 through 1972. Various
issues.

TANU, *"Taarifa ya Ofisi Kuu Kuhusu Hali na Kazi
za Chama.* " November 1967, April 1969, and
1971, and Daily News (Dar es Salaam), June 9,
1975.

TANU. *"The Constitution of TANU, 1973, with
some revisions."* Daily News (Dar es Salaam),
September 30, 1975.
Thayer. L.O. Administrative Communication.
Homewood, Illinois: R.D. Irwin, 1961.

Thomas, Garry. Division of Crop Proceeds, Upper
Kitete Village Settlement 1965/66. Syracuse
University, Village Settlement Project, Report

37, February 28, 1966. *Uhuru* (Dar es Salaam), November 8, 1973.

UNESCO. New Educational Media in Action: Case Studies for Planners. Paris: International Institute for Educational Planning, 1967.

Weiss, W. *"Effects of the Mass Media of Communication."* In Handbook of Social Psychology. Edited by G. Lindzey and E. Aronson. Reading, Massachusetts: Addison-Wesley, 1969.

Wilcox, Dennis L. *"Kenya."* In World Press Encyclopedia. Edited by George Kurian. New York, New York: Facts of File, Inc., 1982.

Wilson, J.F. and Arnold, C.C. *"Public Speaking as a Literal Art."* Boston: Allyn and Bacon, 1964.

Wright, J.S. and Warner, D.S. *"Advertising."* New York: McGraw-Hill, 1962.

Wood, Alan. *"The Groundnut Affair."* London: The Bodley Head, 1950

Yeager, Rodger. *Tanzania: An African Experiment.* Boulder, Colorado: Westview Press, 1982.

Yu, Fredrick T.C. *"Communications and Politics in Communist China." In Communications and Political Development.* Edited by Lucian W. Pye. Princeton, New Jersey: Princeton University Press, 1963.